Crosswalking

Processing MARC in XML Environments with MARC4J

Bas Peters

Crosswalking: Processing MARC in XML Environments with MARC4J

by Bas Peters

Published 2007
Copyright © 2007 by Bas Peters

First edition

ISBN 978-1-84753-028-8

Table of Contents

List of Figures

List of Tables

x

List of Examples

Preface

This concise book is for library programmers who want to learn to use MARC4J to process MARC (Machine Readable Cataloging) data. MARC4J is an open source software library for working with MARC records in Java™, a popular platform independent programming language. The MARC format was originally designed to enable the exchange of bibliographic data between computer systems by providing a structure and format for the storage of bibliographic records on half-inch magnetic tape. Though today most records are transferred by other media, the exchange format has not changed since its first release in 1967 and is still widely used worldwide. At the same time, there is a growing interest in the use of XML in libraries, mainly because the web is moving towards a platform- and application-independent interface for information services, with XML as its universal data format.

MARC4J is designed to bridge the gap between MARC and XML. The software library has built-in support for reading and writing MARC and MARCXML data, thus providing a programming environment for crosswalking: take records in one bibliographic format as input and output these records in a different format. MARC4J also provides a pipeline to enable MARC records to go through further transformations using XSLT to convert MARC records to MODS (Metadata Object Description Schema), Dublin Core or any other bibliographic format. This feature is particularly useful since there is currently no agreed-upon standard for XML in library applications.

Although MARC4J can be used as a command-line tool for conversions between MARC and XML, its main goal is to provide an Application Programming Interface (API) to develop any kind of Java program or servlet that involves reading or writing MARC data. The core piece is a MARC reader that hides the complexity of the MARC record by providing a simple interface to extract information from MARC records. Support for XML is implemented using the standard Java XML interfaces as specified in Sun's Java API for XML Processing (JAXP). By limiting itself to the JAXP API, MARC4J is XML processor-independent and easy to integrate in applications that build on industry standards such as SAX (Simple API for XML), DOM (Document Object Model) or XSLT.

What You Should Already Know

This book assumes that you are interested in developing Java applications that involve MARC data or one of the MARC related XML standards like MARCXML or MODS. You have a basic understanding of a MARC format like MARC 21 or UNIMARC and are familiar with the basics of XML and related standards like XML Namespaces and XSLT. Working with MARC4J does not require exceptional skills in Java programming. The API is designed to be easy to learn and easy to use and this book provides numerous examples. If you have no experience with the Java programming language at all, you should start with getting familiar with the basic concepts of the language. The Tutorials and Online Training section on the Sun Developer Network (SDN) provides some good introductory tutorials on the Java programming language.

Organization of This Book

This book is divided into the following chapters:

Chapter 1, *Reading Data*
Chapter 1 provides a short introduction about MARC formats and then focuses on reading MARC and MARCXML data. This chapter also explains how to create and update records and how to pre-process the input to convert MODS to MARC.

Chapter 2, *Writing Data*
Chapter 2 concentrates on the details of writing MARC and MARCXML data and how to post-process the output to convert MARC to MODS.

Chapter 3, *MARC4J and JAXP*
Chapter 3 explores integration with some important Java XML API's including JAXP, SAX and DOM. It demonstrates how to write the result to a DOM document, how to format XML output using a dedicated XML serializer, how to build pipelines using XSLT and how to use the SAX interface as an alternative to XSLT.

Chapter 4, *Indexing with Lucene*
Chapter 4 concentrates on indexing and searching MARC data with Apache Lucene using the MARC4J Lucene API.

Chapter 5, *Putting It All Together*
Chapter 5 focuses on building an SRU Search/Retrieve web application using the various MARC4J interfaces and classes to process MARC data and using Lucene for indexing and searching.

Appendix A, *MARC4J API Summary*
Appendix A provides a summary of the core MARC4J interfaces and classes.

Appendix B, *Command-line Reference*
Appendix B documents the command-line programs included in the MARC4J API.

Conventions Used in This Book

The following conventions are used in this book.

Typographic Conventions

`method()`
> Used for method names.

`class, interface or package`
> Used for names identifying classes, interfaces and packages.

element, attribute
> Used for XML mark-up.

command
> Used for commands.

parameter
> Used for replaceable items in code and text.

`file`
> Used for file and directory names.

Icons

Note

This icon designates a note relating to the surrounding text.

Tip

This icon designates a helpful tip relating to the surrounding text.

Warning

This icon designates a warning relating to the surrounding text.

Getting the Software

You can download a MARC4J distribution at http://marc4j.tigris.org. On the project home page you can find a direct link to the latest release. You can also find links to MARC4J distributions on the Documents & Files page. A link to this page can be found in the Project Tools menu. The latest version at the time of this writing was MARC4J 2.3.1. The download includes Javadoc documentation, source code and two JAR files: `marc4j.jar` and `normalizer.jar`. Add both files to your CLASSPATH environment variable.

Note

Starting from release 2.0, MARC4J was completely rebuilt. The 2.0 and later releases are not compatible with older versions of MARC4J. The event based parser in the older versions is replaced by an easier to use interface that uses a simple iterator over a collection of MARC records.

MARC4J requires Java 2 Standard Edition (J2SE) 1.4 or later because it requires the `java.util.regex` package to provide support for regular expressions. Some classes contained in this package are used by the `find()` methods introduced in MARC4J version 2.1. The J2SE distribution already contains the JAXP and SAX2 compliant XML parser and XSLT processor required by MARC4J, but you can use a different implementation.

Getting Examples from This Book

Most of the examples from chapter 1, 2 and 3 are available in the package `org.marc4j.samples` of the MARC4J distribution. Look in the `src` directory in the distribution for the Java source code. The SRU Search/Retrieve web application from chapter 5 is available for download from the Documents & Files section of the MARC4J project site (http://marc4j.tigris.org).

Acknowledgments

The first published version of MARC4J was released in February 2002 as James (Java MARC Events). The name of the library changed to MARC4J when the project was accepted by Tigris.org, an open source community for Software Engineering Tools hosted by Collabnet. Originally the library provided an event based parser like the SAX (Simple API for XML) interface, but for release 2.0 the parser was rewritten to provide an easier to use interface.

Acknowledgments

A problem with open source software is that you do not exactly know who your users are. I received questions and bug fixes from developers from all over the world. Although MARC has been declared dead several times, this shows that the standard is still used in many countries. At the same time a growing number of libraries are migrating their bibliographic data to other environments to transform their call-number lookup systems into 21st century resource discovery systems. MARC4J has proved to be a helpful tool in these environments.

I'd like to thank all the contributors who helped me to improve MARC4J. I haven't been involved in library programming in recent years, but I am still committed to continue development of MARC4J, although it is sometimes difficult to find time.

This book contains many references to the Library of Congress, the agency that maintains most of the standards implemented by MARC4J, but neither this book nor the MARC4J software is by any means affiliated with this institution.

Chapter 1. Reading Data

MARC Formats

MARC records consist of structure, markup and content. These components are specified in MARC formats. The first MARC format was developed by the Library of Congress in the sixties for the exchange of bibliographic data using half-inch magnetic tape. Work on the standard was directed towards the development of an international standard, but most countries have since developed national formats. To enable the exchange of bibliographic records between national agencies, the UNIMARC standard was developed. The first UNIMARC edition was published in 1977. Since 1997 the national formats used by the United States (USMARC), Canada (CANMARC) and the United Kingdom (UKMARC) are merged into the MARC 21 standard.

The structure of all MARC records is based on an exchange format for bibliographic records as specified in the ANSI/NISO Z39.2 and ISO 2709:1996 standards. The markup and content is different for the different national formats and reflects the standards used related to cataloging like cataloging rules, classification scheme's and subject headings. Since all MARC formats use the same structure, MARC4J should have no problem reading them. The examples in this book are based on the MARC 21 format.

The structure of a MARC record is pretty straightforward, but it is not human-readable. It consists of a byte stream with four building blocks:

Leader
> The leader is a fixed length field of 24 characters containing record processing information like the record length, the status of the record, the type of material being cataloged and the base address of data. The base address of data is the starting position for the variable fields.

Directory
> The directory immediately follows the leader and provides an index to the fields. For each field the directory provides an entry containing the field identifier or tag (three digits), the field length (four digits) and the starting position (five digits). The directory is terminated by a field separator. The following example is a single directory entry:

```
245007800172
```

In this example a variable field identified by tag 245 has a length of 78 characters and starts at character position 172 relative to the base address of data.

Variable Fields

The variable fields containing the actual record content follow after the directory. There are three kinds of variable fields:

- control number field (a special control field identified by tag 001)

- control fields (identified by tags 002 through 009)

- data fields (identified by tags 010 through 999)

Each variable field is terminated by a field separator. The control number field should always be the first field. Control fields contain only data, but the structure of a data field is slightly more complex. A data field can contain indicators and subfields. Indicators are single character data elements that can contain additional data for a field. In MARC 21, for example, fields with title information use an indicator for the number of non-filing characters to enable a computer program to ignore articles. A subfield is identified by a single character, called a data element identifier or subfield code, preceded by a subfield delimiter.

The example which follows represents a data field for tag 245 (title statement). The dollar sign represents a subfield delimiter. The two digits following the tag are the indicator values. The first indicator indicates that a title added entry is to be generated from this field and the second indicator specifies the number of non-filing characters. This field has two subfields. Subfield $a contains the title proper and subfield $c the statement of responsibility.

```
245 10$aSummerland /$cMichael Chabon.
```

Record Terminator

The record terminator is the final character of the record.

The MARC4J API is not a full implementation of the ANSI/NISO Z39.2 or ISO 2709:1996 standard. The standard is implemented as it is used in the different MARC formats. The MARC4J parser assumes that there are 2 indicators and that the subfield code length is 2. Subrecords are not supported.

The use of MARC4J is not limited to records in ISO 2709 format. MARC4J can handle all kinds of bibliographic XML formats, like MODS and Dublin Core, through MARCXML that serves as an intermediary format. It is also possible to implement the interfaces used for reading and writing data to provide support for other bibliographic formats.

Introducing MARC4J

For reading MARC data, MARC4J provides implementations of an interface called `MarcReader`. This interface has two methods that provide an iterator to read MARC data from an input source:

`hasNext()`
> Returns `true` if the iteration has more records, `false` otherwise.

`next()`
> Returns the next record in the iteration as a `Record` object.

If you are familiar with the Java Collections Framework you might have used iterators. When you have a `List` in Java, you can access the items on the list through an `Iterator` that can be obtained from the `List` object:

```
Iterator i = list.iterator();
while (i.hasNext()) {
    Object item = i.next();
    // do something with the item object
}
```

Tip

It is recommended to have the Java 2 Standard Edition (J2SE) documentation at hand when programming with MARC4J. MARC4J uses standard Java language features where possible, making it an easy API to work with for Java developers. The J2SE documentation is available on Sun's Developer Network (SDN) site.

MARC4J provides two classes that implement `MarcReader`:

`MarcStreamReader`
> An iterator over a collection of MARC records in ISO 2709 format.

`MarcXmlReader`
> An iterator over a collection of MARC records in MARCXML format.

Let's start with reading MARC records in ISO 2709 format. To do this you need to import three MARC4J classes:

```
import org.marc4j.MarcReader;
import org.marc4j.MarcStreamReader;
import org.marc4j.marc.Record;
```

The `MarcReader` interface and the `MarcStreamReader` class are required to read MARC data. The `Record` interface provides an in-memory representation of a MARC record. To read MARC data you need an input stream to read records from, for example one that reads input from a local file:

```
InputStream in = new FileInputStream("summerland.mrc");
```

You can instantiate an `InputStream` using a `File` object:

```
File file = new File("/Users/bpeters/Documents", "summerland.mrc");
InputStream in = new FileInputStream(file);
```

Once you have an input stream, you can initialize the `MarcReader` implementation:

```
MarcReader reader = new MarcStreamReader(in);
```

It is possible to read directly from a URL using the `java.net.URL` class:

```
URL url = new URL(
  "http://www.loc.gov/standards/marcxml/Sandburg/sandburg.mrc");

MarcReader reader = new MarcStreamReader(url.openStream());
```

After instantiating a `MarcReader` implementation, you can start reading records from the input stream.

```
while (reader.hasNext()) {
    Record record = reader.next();

}
```

If you want to examine the records, you can write each record to standard output using the toString() method:

```
System.out.println(record.toString());
```

Example 1.1, "Reading MARC Data" shows the complete program. It reads records from a file summerland.mrc located in the current directory and writes each record to standard output using the toString() method.

Example 1.1. Reading MARC Data

```
import org.marc4j.MarcReader;
import org.marc4j.MarcStreamReader;
import org.marc4j.marc.Record;
import java.io.InputStream;
import java.io.FileInputStream;

public class ReadMarcExample {

    public static void main(String args[]) throws Exception {

        InputStream in = new FileInputStream("summerland.mrc");
        MarcReader reader = new MarcStreamReader(in);
        while (reader.hasNext()) {
            Record record = reader.next();
            System.out.println(record.toString());
        }

    }

}
```

When you compile and run this program, it will write each record in tagged display format to standard output, like this:

```
LEADER 00714cam a2200205 a 4500
001 12883376
005 20030616111422.0
008 020805s2002    nyu    j       000 1 eng
020    $a0786803772
020    $a0786815155 (pbk.)
040    $aDLC$cDLC$dDLC
100 1 $aChabon, Michael.
245 10$aSummerland /$cMichael Chabon.
250    $a1st ed.
260    $aNew York :$bMiramax Books/Hyperion Books for Children,$cc2002.
300    $a500 p. ;$c22 cm.
520    $aEthan Feld, the worst baseball player in the history of the game,
   finds himself recruited by a 100-year-old scout to help a band of
   fairies triumph over an ancient enemy.
650    1$aFantasy.
650    1$aBaseball$vFiction.
650    1$aMagic$vFiction.
```

Note

The record for *Summerland* by Michael Chabon is used as an example throughout this book. The cataloging agency is the Library of Congress.

When instantiating a MarcStreamReader, it is possible to add the character encoding as an argument. MARC4J reads ISO 2709 records as binary data, but data elements in control fields and subfields are converted to String values. When Java decodes a byte array to a String, it needs a character encoding. The default encoding used by MarcStreamReader is ISO 8859-1 (Latin 1). Most character encodings used in MARC formats are 8-bits encodings, like ISO 8859-1, but encodings such as MARC-8 are not directly supported by Java. When parsing MARC 21 data, MarcStreamReader tries to detect the encoding from the character coding scheme in the leader (character position 9). If the value is 'a', UTF-8 is used, otherwise the reader uses the default encoding. You can always override the default encoding when instantiating a MarcStreamReader using a Java encoding name:

```
// decode data elements as UTF-8
MarcReader reader = new MarcStreamReader(in, "UTF8");
```

```
// decode data elements as Latin-2
MarcReader reader = new MarcStreamReader(in, "ISO8859_2");

// decode data elements as KOI8-R, Russian
MarcReader reader = new MarcStreamReader(in, "KOI8_R");
```

It is not required to read records from an input stream using a `while()` loop. If you know that your input data only contains a single record, you can simply read the record using the `next()` method:

```
MarcReader reader = new MarcStreamReader(input);
Record record = reader.next();
System.out.println(record.toString());
```

You can check for a record using an if statement:

```
MarcReader reader = new MarcStreamReader(input);

if (reader.hasNext()) {
    Record record = reader.next();
    System.out.println(record.toString());
} else {
    System.err.println("Reader has no record.");
}
```

This can be useful when a different class reads each single record as a byte stream. You can then create a `ByteArrayInputStream` using the constructor that takes a byte array as a parameter and use that to initialize the `MarcReader` implementation. Let's assume that we have a byte array *bytes* containing the byte stream for a single record in ISO 2709 format. The following listing shows how you can create a `Record` instance from this byte array:

```
// we have a byte array called bytes
InputStream in = new ByteArrayInputStream(bytes);

MarcReader reader = new MarcStreamReader(in);
if (reader.hasNext()) {
    Record record = reader.next();
```

```
    System.out.println(record.toString());
} else {
    System.err.println("Reader has no record.");
}
```

When a `MarcReader` implementation encounters a parse error, a `MarcException` is thrown by the reader. This is an unchecked exception that you are not required to catch. If however you want to recover errors in your application, you can add exception handling by adding a try and catch block to your code:

```
try {
    MarcReader reader = new MarcStreamReader(input);
    Record record = reader.next();
    System.out.println(record.toString());
} catch (MarcException e) {
    System.err.println("exception thrown");
}
```

The Record Object Model

The `Record` interface is the root of the record object model implemented by MARC4J. It provides access to the leader and variable fields. You can use it to read, add, move or remove data elements contained in the leader and variable fields. The record object model is implemented in the `org.marc4j.marc` package. The core interfaces are `Record`, `Leader`, `VariableField`, `ControlField`, `DataField` and `Subfield`. This section covers the most important interfaces and methods the record object model provides. Check Appendix A, *MARC4J API Summary* for a complete overview.

The following method returns the leader:

```
Leader leader = record.getLeader();
```

The `Leader` interface provides access to all the leader values. While the Leader represents most y MARC structural information, some character positions provide useful bibliographic information. The method `getTypeOfRecord()`, for example, identifies the type of material being cataloged, such as language material, cartographic material, musical sound recording, or computer file.

There are several methods available to retrieve variable fields. The method getVariableFields() returns all variable fields as a List object, but in most cases you will use methods that provide more control. The following method returns all control fields:

```
// returns fields for tags 001 through 009
List fields = record.getControlFields();
```

And this method returns all data fields:

```
// returns fields for tags 010 through 999
List fields = record.getDataFields();
```

Both ControlField and DataField are sub-interfaces of the VariableField interface that provides access to the tag through the getTag() method. For control fields MARC4J does not provide you with the level of detail you might expect. You can retrieve the data using the getData() mehod. To retrieve specific data elements at character positions, you need to use some standard Java. This is because MARC4J is designed to handle different MARC formats like MARC 21 and UNIMARC. To retrieve a data element in a control field, such as the language of the item, you can do something like this:

```
// get control field with tag 008
ControlField field = (ControlField) record.getVariableField("008");
String data = field.getData();

// the three-character MARC language code takes character positions 35-37
String lang = data.substring(35,38);
System.out.println("Language: " + lang);
```

For the *Summerland* record used in Example 1.1, "Reading MARC Data", this code would produce the following output:

```
Language: eng
```

MARC4J provides two methods to read the control number. Use the method `getControlNumberField()` to retrieve the `ControlField` instance for tag 001, or use `getControlNumber()` to retrieve the control number as a `String` object.

The code listing that demonstrated how to retrieve the language also showed how you can retrieve variable fields for a given tag using the `getVariableField(String tag)` method. There are several methods to retrieve specific fields. Use `getVariableField(String tag)` to retrieve the first field occurrence for a given tag:

```
DataField title = (DataField) record.getVariableField("245");
```

Use `getVariableFields(String tag)` to retrieve all occurrences:

```
List subjects = record.getVariableFields("650");
```

You can add multiple tag values using a `String` array as an argument:

```
String[] tags = {"010", "100", "245", "250", "260", "300"};
List fields = record.getVariableFields(tags);
```

These methods return instances of `VariableField`, so if you need to access methods that are specific to the `ControlField` or `DataField` interface, you need to cast the instance of `VariableField` to the specific subclass:

```
// cast a variable field to a control field
ControlField field = (ControlField) record.getVariableField("008");

// cast a variable field to a data field
DataField field = (DataField) record.getVariableField("245");
```

Where the `ControlField` interface requires only one method to retrieve the data element, the `DataField` interface is slightly more complex, since it has indicators and subfields. You can retrieve the indicators using the `getIndicator1()` and `getIndicator2()` methods. Subfields are represented by the `Subfield` interface. The

The Record Object Model

Subfield interface has a `getCode()` method to retrieve the subfield code and a `getData()` method to retrieve the data element.

The following code listing retrieves the title information field and writes the tag, indicators and subfields to standard output:

```
DataField field = (DataField) record.getVariableField("245");

String tag = field.getTag();
char ind1 = field.getIndicator1();
char ind2 = field.getIndicator2();

System.out.println("Tag: " + tag + " Indicator 1: " + ind1 +
    " Indicator 2: " + ind2);

List subfields = field.getSubfields();
Iterator i = subfields.iterator();

while (i.hasNext()) {

    Subfield subfield = (Subfield) i.next();
    char code = subfield.getCode();
    String data = subfield.getData();

    System.out.println("Subfield code: " + code +
        " Data element: " + data);

}
```

For the *Summerland* record, this would produce the following output:

```
Tag: 245 Indicator 1: 1 Indicator 2: 0
Subfield code: a Data element: Summerland /
Subfield code: c Data element: Michael Chabon.
```

The DataField interface also provides methods to retrieve specific subfields:

```
// retrieve the first occurrence of subfield with code 'a'
Subfield subfield = field.getSubfield('a');
```

```
// retrieve all subfields with code 'a'
List subfields = field.getSubfields('a');
```

The following listing uses `getSubfield(char code)` to retrieve the title proper. It then removes the non-sort characters:

```
// get data field 245
DataField field = (DataField) record.getVariableField("245");

// get indicator 2
char ind2 = field.getIndicator2();

// get the title proper
Subfield subfield = field.getSubfield('a');
String title = subfield.getData();

// remove the non sorting characters
int nonSort = Character.digit(ind2, 10);
title = title.substring(nonSort);
```

In addition to retrieving fields by tag name, you can also retrieve fields by data element values using the `find()` methods. The search capabilities are limited, but they can be useful when processing records. This method call retrieves all fields that contain the text 'Chabon':

```
List fields = record.find("Chabon");
```

You can add a tag value to limit the result to a particular tag. The following example limits the fields that are searched to the title statement:

```
List fields = record.find("245", "Summerland");
```

You can add multiple tag values using a `String` array. To find 'Graham, Paul' in main or added entries for a personal name:

```
String tags = {"100", "600"};
List fields = record.find(tags, "Graham, Paul")
```

The `find()` method is also useful if you need to retrieve records that meet certain criteria, such as a specific control number, title words or a particular publisher or subject. Example 1.2, "A Check Agency Program" shows a complete example. It checks if the cataloging agency is DLC. It also shows how you can extend the find capabilities to specific subfields. This feature is not directly available in MARC4J, since it is easy to accomplish using the record object model together with the standard Java API's.

Example 1.2. A Check Agency Program

```java
import java.io.InputStream;
import java.io.FileInputStream;
import org.marc4j.MarcReader;
import org.marc4j.MarcStreamReader;
import org.marc4j.marc.Record;
import org.marc4j.marc.DataField;
import java.util.List;

public class CheckAgencyExample {

    public static void main(String args[]) throws Exception {

        InputStream input = new FileInputStream("file.mrc");

        MarcReader reader = new MarcStreamReader(input);
        while (reader.hasNext()) {
            Record record = reader.next();

            // check if the cataloging agency is DLC
            List result = record.find("040", "DLC");
            if (result.size() > 0)
                System.out.println("Agency for this record is DLC");

            // it is not possible to specify a subfield code
            // so to check if it is the original cataloging agency
            DataField field = (DataField)result.get(0);
            String agency = field.getSubfield('a').getData();
```

```
        if (agency.matches("DLC"))
            System.out.println("DLC is the original agency");
    }
  }

}
```

By using `find()` you can also implement search and replace functionalities to batch update records that meet certain criteria. You can use Java regular expressions. Check the `java.util.regex` package for more information and examples about pattern matching. *Mastering Regular Expressions* by Jeffrey E.F. Friedl is an excellent book if you want to learn more about regular expressions. It also covers the `java.util.regex` package.

Creating and Updating Records

You can use the record object model to create or update records. This is done using the `MarcFactory`. This class provides a number of helper methods to create instances of `Record`, `Leader`, `ControlField`, `DataField` and `Subfield` implementations. The following listing demonstrates some of the features `MarcFactory` provides by creating a minimal level record from scratch. It contains the control number field and a single data field holding the title proper and statement of responsibility.

```
// create a factory instance
MarcFactory factory = MarcFactory.newInstance();

// create a record with leader
Record record = factory.newRecord("00000cam a2200000 a 4500");

// add a control field
record.addVariableField(factory.newControlField("001", "12883376"));

// create a data field
DataField dataField = factory.newDataField("245", '1', '0');
dataField.addSubfield(factory.newSubfield('a', "Summerland /"));
dataField.addSubfield(factory.newSubfield('c', "Michael Chabon."));

// add the data field to the record
record.addVariableField(dataField);
```

14

The main purpose of the `MarcFactory` class is to enable you to update existing records. In Example 1.3, "Add Electronic Location" it is used to add an electronic location to the *Summerland* record.

Example 1.3. Add Electronic Location

```
import java.io.InputStream;
import java.io.FileInputStream;
import org.marc4j.MarcReader;
import org.marc4j.MarcStreamReader;
import org.marc4j.marc.DataField;
import org.marc4j.marc.MarcFactory;
import org.marc4j.marc.Record;

public class AddLocationExample {

    public static void main(String args[]) throws Exception {

        InputStream in = new FileInputStream("summerland.mrc");

        MarcFactory factory = MarcFactory.newInstance();

        MarcReader reader = new MarcStreamReader(in);
        while (reader.hasNext()) {
            Record record = reader.next();

            DataField field = factory.newDataField("856", '4', '2');

            field.addSubfield(factory.newSubfield('3',
                "Contributor biographical information"));

            field.addSubfield(factory.newSubfield('u',
                "http://en.wikipedia.org/wiki/Michael_Chabon"));

            record.addVariableField(field);

            System.out.println(record.toString());
        }
    }

}
```

In this example, the `MarcFactory` instance is used to create the `DataField` and the two subfields containing the data elements for the electronic location. The new data field is then added to the `Record` instance. When you compile and run this program, it will write the *Summerland* record to standard output with the new field containing the reference to the biographical information about the author:

```
LEADER 00714cam a2200205 a 4500
001 12883376
005 20030616111422.0
008 020805s2002    nyu    j       000 1 eng
020    $a0786808772
020    $a0786816155 (pbk.)
040    $aDLC$cDLC$dDLC
100 1 $aChabon, Michael.
245 10$aSummerland /$cMichael Chabon.
250    $a1st ed.
260    $aNew York :$bMiramax Books/Hyperion Books for Children,$cc2002.
300    $a500 p. ;$c22 cm.
520    $aEthan Feld, the worst baseball player in the history of the game,
   finds himself recruited by a 100-year-old scout to help a band of
   fairies triumph over an ancient enemy.
650    1$aFantasy.
650    1$aBaseball$vFiction.
650    1$aMagic$vFiction.
856 42$3Contributor biographical information$uhttp://en.wikipedia.org/
   wiki/Michael_Chabon
```

Since one of the design goals of the record object model was to keep the interface as simple as possible, there are no specific methods to execute such operations as removing fields based on particular conditions. This means that you have to write such methods yourself. Example 1.4, "Remove Local Fields" removes all local fields (tags 9XX) from the record read from the input stream. It will first write the original record to standard output and then the updated record without the local fields.

Example 1.4. Remove Local Fields

```
import java.io.InputStream;
import java.io.FileInputStream;
import java.util.Iterator;
import java.util.List;
```

```
import java.util.regex.Matcher;
import java.util.regex.Pattern;
import org.marc4j.MarcReader;
import org.marc4j.MarcStreamReader;
import org.marc4j.marc.DataField;
import org.marc4j.marc.Record;

public class RemoveLocalFieldsExample {

    public static void main(String args[]) throws Exception {

        InputStream in = new FileInputStream("summerland.mrc");

        Pattern pattern = Pattern.compile("9\\d\\d");

        MarcReader reader = new MarcStreamReader(input);
        while (reader.hasNext()) {
            Record record = reader.next();

            System.out.println(record.toString());

            List fields = record.getDataFields();

            Iterator i = fields.iterator();
            while (i.hasNext()) {
                DataField field = (DataField) i.next();
                Matcher matcher = pattern.matcher(field.getTag());
                if (matcher.matches())
                    i.remove();
            }

            System.out.println(record.toString());
        }

    }
}
```

A regular expression is used to match all tags that start with a 9 followed by two digits:

```
Pattern pattern = Pattern.compile("9\\d\\d");
```

The `getDataFields()` method returns the `List` instance that holds the `DataField` objects for the record, so you can directly manipulate this list using the `Iterator` class. Each tag in the list of data fields is matched against the pattern. If there is a match, the field is removed from the list using the `Iterator.remove()` method:

```
Matcher matcher = pattern.matcher(field.getTag());
if (matcher.matches())
    i.remove();
```

You can directly manipulate the `List` objects returned by the `getControlFields()` and `getDataFields()` methods, but you cannot directly manipulate the `List` object returned by the `getVariableFields()` method. You can use the method `removeVariableField(VariableField)` in these cases.

Reading MARCXML Data

Until now we have been processing MARC data in ISO 2709 format, but you can also read MARC data in MARCXML format. The MARC 21 XML schema was published in June 2002 by the Library of Congress to encourage the standardization of MARC 21 records in XML environments. The schema was developed in collaboration with OCLC and RLG after a survey of schema's that were used in various projects trying to bridge the gap between MARC and XML, including a MARCXML schema developed by the OAI (Open Archives Initiative) and the one used in early releases of MARC4J. The MARCXML schema is specified in a W3C XML Schema and provides lossless conversion between MARC ISO 2709 and MARCXML. As a consequence, information in a MARCXML record enables recreation of a MARC ISO 2709 record without loss of data. Figure 1.1, "MARCXML Record" shows the record for *Summerland* by Michael Chabon in MARCXML:

Figure 1.1. MARCXML Record

```
<?xml version="1.0" encoding="UTF-8"?>
<collection xmlns="http://www.loc.gov/MARC21/slim">
  <record>
    <leader>00714cam a2200205 a 4500</leader>
    <controlfield tag="001">12883376</controlfield>
    <controlfield tag="005">20030616111422.0</controlfield>
    <controlfield tag="008">020805s2002    nyu    j        0
00 1 eng  </controlfield>
```

```
<datafield tag="020" ind1=" " ind2=" ">
 <subfield code="a">0786808772</subfield>
</datafield>
<datafield tag="020" ind1=" " ind2=" ">
 <subfield code="a">0786816155 (pbk.)</subfield>
</datafield>
<datafield tag="040" ind1=" " ind2=" ">
 <subfield code="a">DLC</subfield>
 <subfield code="c">DLC</subfield>
 <subfield code="d">DLC</subfield>
</datafield>
<datafield tag="100" ind1="1" ind2=" ">
 <subfield code="a">Chabon, Michael.</subfield>
</datafield>
<datafield tag="245" ind1="1" ind2="0">
 <subfield code="a">Summerland /</subfield>
 <subfield code="c">Michael Chabon.</subfield>
</datafield>
<datafield tag="250" ind1=" " ind2=" ">
 <subfield code="a">1st ed.</subfield>
</datafield>
<datafield tag="260" ind1=" " ind2=" ">
 <subfield code="a">New York :</subfield>
 <subfield code="b">Miramax Books/Hyperion Books for
Children,</subfield>
 <subfield code="c">c2002.</subfield>
</datafield>
<datafield tag="300" ind1=" " ind2=" ">
 <subfield code="a">500 p. ;</subfield>
 <subfield code="c">22 cm.</subfield>
</datafield>
<datafield tag="520" ind1=" " ind2=" ">
 <subfield code="a">Ethan Feld, the worst baseball player in the
history of the game, finds himself recruited by a 100-year-old scout
to help a band of fairies triumph over an ancient enemy.</subfield>
</datafield>
<datafield tag="650" ind1=" " ind2="1">
 <subfield code="a">Fantasy.</subfield>
</datafield>
<datafield tag="650" ind1=" " ind2="1">
 <subfield code="a">Baseball</subfield>
 <subfield code="v">Fiction.</subfield>
</datafield>
<datafield tag="650" ind1=" " ind2="1">
 <subfield code="a">Magic</subfield>
```

```
        <subfield code="v">Fiction.</subfield>
      </datafield>
    </record>
</collection>
```

As you can see the markup and content are still the same. The variable fields have tags and the data fields have indicators and subfields identified by a code. The only difference from the record in ISO 2709 format is that the MARCXML record is structured using XML markup. There is even data present that has no meaning outside the ISO 2709 format, like the record length and the base address of data in the leader. A MARCXML record is more readable than a record in ISO 2709 format, but it is still not very user friendly, because it uses the numeric tags instead of language-based elements, like for example *title* or *subject*. It is not the goal of MARCXML to provide a markup that is end user oriented. The only purpose of MARCXML is to bridge the gap between MARC and XML. Where ISO 2709 is an exchange format, MARCXML is an intermediary format.

Reading MARCXML data is not different from reading MARC data in ISO 2709 format, but the MARCXML reader provides some additional XML related features. Example 1.5, "Reading MARCXML Data" is similar to Example 1.1, "Reading MARC Data", but now reading a file containing records in MARCXML format.

Example 1.5. Reading MARCXML Data

```java
import org.marc4j.MarcReader;
import org.marc4j.MarcXmlReader;
import org.marc4j.marc.Record;
import java.io.InputStream;
import java.io.FileInputStream;

public class ReadMarcXmlExample {

    public static void main(String args[]) throws Exception {

        InputStream in = new FileInputStream("summerland.xml");

        MarcReader reader = new MarcXmlReader(in);

        while (reader.hasNext()) {
            Record record = reader.next();
            System.out.println(record.toString());
```

```
                  }
            }

      }
```

When you compile and run this program, it will write each record in tagged display format to standard output:

```
LEADER 00714cam a2200205 a 4500
001 12883376
005 20030616111422.0
008 020805s2002    nyu    j       000 1 eng
020    $a0786808772
020    $a0786816155 (pbk.)
040    $aDLC$cDLC$dDLC
100 1 $aChabon, Michael.
245 10$aSummerland /$cMichael Chabon.
250    $a1st ed.
260    $aNew York :$bMiramax Books/Hyperion Books for Children,$cc2002.
300    $a500 p. ;$c22 cm.
520    $aEthan Feld, the worst baseball player in the history of the
   game, finds himself recruited by a 100-year-old scout to help a
   band of fairies triumph over an ancient enemy.
650    1$aFantasy.
650    1$aBaseball$vFiction.
650    1$aMagic$vFiction.
```

Instead of using an instance of InputStream, you can create a MarcXmlReader using an instance of InputSource. The InputSource class is part of the SAX (Simple API for XML) interface. It has several constructors to provide input data to the underlying XML parser that is used to create Record objects from the MARCXML document. The following list summarizes the most important features:

InputSource(String)
> Use this constructor to provide data from a fully qualified URI, including *http://*, *file://* or *ftp://*.

InputSource(java.io.Reader)
> Use this constructor to provide pre-decoded data to the parser. The parser will ignore the character encoding in the XML declaration.

21

`InputSource(java.io.InputStream)`
 Use this constructor to provide binary data to the parser. The parser will then try to detect the encoding from the binary data or the XML declaration.

`InputSource.setEncoding(String)`
 Use this method to specify the character encoding of the XML data that is provided to the parser.

Example 1.6, "Reading MARCXML from an `InputSource`" reads data from a given HTTP address using a `MarcXmlReader` constructor that takes an instance of `InputSource` as a parameter.

Example 1.6. Reading MARCXML from an `InputSource`

```
import org.marc4j.MarcReader;
import org.marc4j.MarcXmlReader;
import org.marc4j.marc.Record;
import org.xml.sax.InputSource;

public class ReadFromInputSourceExample {

    public static void main(String args[]) throws Exception {

        String systemId =
          "http://www.loc.gov/standards/marcxml/Sandburg/sandburg.xml";

        InputSource input = new InputSource(systemId);

        MarcReader reader = new MarcXmlReader(input);

        while (reader.hasNext()) {
            Record record = reader.next();
            System.out.println(record.toString());
        }

    }

}
```

Reading MODS Data

Let's look at some of the specific XML related features of `MarcXmlReader`. The most interesting feature is that you can pre-process the input using a stylesheet. This enables you to create a stylesheet in XSLT that transforms XML data to MARCXML. You can then process the result like you would do with MARCXML or MARC in ISO 2709 format. To demonstrate this feature we will use MARC4J to create `Record` objects from MODS data.

MODS is a schema for a bibliographic element set that is maintained by the Library of Congress. The schema provides a subset of the MARC standard, but an advantage to the MARCXML format is that it uses language-based tags rather than numeric ones. MODS can carry selected data from existing MARC records, but the standard also enables the creation of original resource description records. The MODS syntax is richer than the Dublin Core element set, but it is simpler to apply than the full MARC 21 bibliographic format. Figure 1.2, "MODS Record" shows a bibliographic record for *Summerland* by Michael Chabon in MODS.

Figure 1.2. MODS Record

```
<?xml version="1.0" encoding="UTF-8"?>
<modsCollection xmlns="http://www.loc.gov/mods/v3">
  <mods version="3.0">
    <titleInfo>
      <title>Summerland</title>
    </titleInfo>
    <name type="personal">
      <namePart>Chabon, Michael.</namePart>
      <role>
        <roleTerm authority="marcrelator" type="text">creator</roleTerm>
      </role>
    </name>
    <typeOfResource>text</typeOfResource>
    <originInfo>
      <place>
        <placeTerm type="code" authority="marccountry">nyu</placeTerm>
      </place>
      <place>
        <placeTerm type="text">New York</placeTerm>
      </place>
      <publisher>Miramax Books/Hyperion Books for Children</publisher>
      <dateIssued>c2002</dateIssued>
```

```
      <dateIssued encoding="marc">2002</dateIssued>
      <edition>1st ed.</edition>
      <issuance>monographic</issuance>
    </originInfo>
    <language>
      <languageTerm authority="iso639-2b" type="code">eng</languageTerm>
    </language>
    <physicalDescription>
      <form authority="marcform">print</form>
      <extent>500 p. ; 22 cm.</extent>
    </physicalDescription>
    <abstract>Ethan Feld, the worst baseball player in the history of
 the game, finds himself recruited by a 100-year-old scout to help a
 band of fairies triumph over an ancient enemy.</abstract>
      <targetAudience authority="marctarget">juvenile</targetAudience>
      <note type="statement of responsibility">Michael Chabon.</note>
      <subject>
        <topic>Fantasy</topic>
      </subject>
      <subject>
        <topic>Baseball</topic>
        <topic>Fiction</topic>
      </subject>
      <subject>
        <topic>Magic</topic>
        <topic>Fiction</topic>
      </subject>
      <identifier type="isbn">0786808772</identifier>
      <identifier type="isbn">0786816155 (pbk.)</identifier>
      <recordInfo>
        <recordContentSource authority="marcorg">DLC</recordContentSource>
        <recordCreationDate encoding="marc">020805</recordCreationDate>
        <recordIdentifier>12883376</recordIdentifier>
      </recordInfo>
    </mods>
</modsCollection>
```

The Library of Congress provides a stylesheet that transforms MODS to MARCXML. Using this stylesheet you can process the bibliographic information contained in a collection of MODS records as MARC data. To do this, you need to add the stylesheet location as an argument when you create the `MarcXmlReader` instance. Example 1.7, "Reading MODS Data" shows the code to create `Record` objects from MODS input.

Example 1.7. Reading MODS Data

```
import org.marc4j.MarcReader;
import org.marc4j.MarcXmlReader;
import org.marc4j.marc.Record;
import java.io.InputStream;
import java.io.FileInputStream;

public class ModsToMarc21Example {

    public static void main(String args[]) throws Exception {

        String stylesheetUrl =
          "http://www.loc.gov/standards/marcxml/xslt/MODS2MARC21slim.xsl";

        InputStream in = new FileInputStream("mods.xml");
        MarcReader reader = new MarcXmlReader(in, stylesheetUrl);
        while (reader.hasNext()) {
            Record record = reader.next();
            System.out.println(record.toString());
        }

    }

}
```

The *stylesheetUrl* variable contains a reference to the location of the XSLT stylesheet. It is passed as an argument on creation of the MarcXmlReader. The reader first transforms the MODS data to MARCXML using the given stylesheet. The XSLT output is then parsed by the MarcXmlReader to create Record objects. When you compile and run this program, it will write the converted data from the MODS document to standard output:

```
LEADER 00000nam  2200000uu 4500
001 12883376
005 20030616111422.0
008 020805|2002    nyu||||j |||||||||||eng||
020   $a0786808772
020   $a0786816155 (pbk.)
```

```
040    $aDLC
100 1 $aChabon, Michael.$ecreator
245 10$aSummerland$cMichael Chabon.
250    $a1st ed
260    $aNew York$bMiramax Books/Hyperion Books for Children$cc2002$c2002
300    $a500 p. ; 22 cm.
520    $aEthan Feld, the worst baseball player in the history of the
  game, finds himself recruited by a 100-year-old scout to help a band
  of fairies triumph over an ancient enemy.
650 1 $aFantasy
650 1 $aBaseball$xFiction
650 1 $aMagic$xFiction
```

In addition to the stylesheet to transform MODS data to MARCXML, the Library of Congress provides the following stylesheets that transform different bibliographic formats to MARCXML:

Dublin Core to MARCXML Stylesheet

The Dublin Core metadata standard is a simple element set for describing a wide range of networked resources. The Dublin Core basic element set comprises fifteen elements such as title, creator, publisher, date, description, subject and identifier. Each element is optional and may be repeated.

OAI MARC to MARCXML Stylesheet

The OAI (Open Archives Initiative) MARC schema was developed for the exchange of MARC records using OAI protocols.

ONIX to MARCXML Stylesheet

The ONIX schema is an international standard for representing and communicating book industry product information in electronic form.

MARC DTD to MARCXML Stylesheet

The MARC DTD's were developed in the mid 1990's to support the conversion of MARC data to SGML (Structured Generalized Markup Language). Although the DTD's have been converted to XML DTD's, they are retired in favor of the MARCXML schema.

You can find the stylesheets at the Tools & Utilities section of the MARCXML standards page. In Chapter 3, *MARC4J and JAXP* we take a closer look at MARC4J in XML environments.

Implementing MarcReader

Sometimes you need to read data that is not in ISO 2709 or a given XML format. In these cases you can implement the `MarcReader` interface to create `Record` objects from an input source. To do this you need to implement two methods:

`hasNext()`

Implement this method to provide an iterator that returns `true` if there are more records available from the input source and `false` when the end of the file is reached.

`next()`

Implement this method to return the next record in the iteration as a `Record` object.

Depending on the data structure you need to parse, writing a custom `MarcReader` implementation can become quite complicated. It is not the goal of this book to teach you how to write parsers in Java, so we will look at a simple implementation. It creates minimal level authority records from a Tab-separated file containing personal names. Each line contains the control number, the personal name and the dates associated with the name. The input file might look like this:

```
34284 Thoreau, Henry David 1817-1862
34542 Hawthorne, Nathaniel 1804-1864
12435 Emerson, Ralph Waldo 1803-1882
```

Since each line contains a record, we can read lines from the input file and then split each line into a list of tokens. We start with the `hasNext()` method. This method should return `true` if there are more lines to read from the reader, or `false` if it reached the end of the file:

```
if ((line = br.readLine()) != null)
    return true;
else
    return false;
```

Each line is then parsed by the `next()` method. The first step is to split the line into tokens. The resulting `String` array should contain three tokens:

```
String[] tokens = line.trim().split("\t");

if (tokens.length != 3)
    throw new MarcException("Invalid number of tokens");
```

You can then use the `MarcFactory` class to create the record object:

```
MarcFactory factory = MarcFactory.newInstance();

Record record = factory.newRecord("00000nz  a2200000o  4500");

ControlField controlField =
    factory.newControlField("001", tokens[0]);

record.addVariableField(controlField);

DataField dataField = factory.newDataField("100", ' ', ' ');
dataField.addSubfield(factory.newSubfield('a', tokens[1]));
dataField.addSubfield(factory.newSubfield('d', tokens[2]));

record.addVariableField(dataField);
```

The code in Example 1.8, "MarcReader Implementation" shows the complete code for the `MarcReader` implementation to parse a Tab-separated file and create minimal level authority records.

Example 1.8. MarcReader Implementation

```
import java.io.BufferedReader;
import java.io.IOException;
import java.io.InputStream;
import java.io.InputStreamReader;

import org.marc4j.MarcException;
import org.marc4j.MarcReader;
import org.marc4j.marc.ControlField;
import org.marc4j.marc.DataField;
import org.marc4j.marc.MarcFactory;
```

```
import org.marc4j.marc.Record;

public class PersonalNamesReader implements MarcReader {

    private BufferedReader br = null;

    private String line;

    public PersonalNamesReader(InputStream in) {
        br = new BufferedReader(new InputStreamReader(in));
    }

    public boolean hasNext() {
        try {
            if ((line = br.readLine()) != null)
                return true;
            else
                return false;
        } catch (IOException e) {
            throw new MarcException(e.getMessage(), e);
        }
    }

    public Record next() {
        String[] tokens = line.trim().split("\t");

        if (tokens.length != 3)
            throw new MarcException("Invalid number of tokens");

        MarcFactory factory = MarcFactory.newInstance();

        Record record = factory.newRecord("00000nz  a2200000o  4500");

        ControlField controlField =
            factory.newControlField("001", tokens[0]);

        record.addVariableField(controlField);

        DataField dataField = factory.newDataField("100", ' ', ' ');
        dataField.addSubfield(factory.newSubfield('a', tokens[1]));
        dataField.addSubfield(factory.newSubfield('d', tokens[2]));

        record.addVariableField(dataField);

        return record;
```

```
        }

    }
```

Using the `PersonalNamesReader` is not different from using the `MarcStreamReader` or `MarcXmlReader` class. Example 1.9, "Driver for PersonalNamesReader" shows the code for a driver to test the `MarcReader` implementation. It reads lines from a file called `names.txt` located in the current directory and writes the authority records to standard output using the `toString()` method.

Example 1.9. Driver for PersonalNamesReader

```
import org.marc4j.MarcReader;
import org.marc4j.marc.Record;
import java.io.InputStream;
import java.io.FileInputStream;

public class ReadPersonalNames {

    public static void main(String args[]) throws Exception {

        InputStream in = new FileInputStream("names.txt");

        MarcReader reader = new PersonalNamesReader(in);

        while (reader.hasNext()) {
            Record record = reader.next();
            System.out.println(record.toString());
        }

    }

}
```

When you compile and run this program, it will write each record in tagged display format to standard output:

```
LEADER 00000nz  a2200000o  4500
001 34284
100 1 $aThoreau, Henry David$d1817-1862

LEADER 00000nz  a2200000o  4500
001 34542
100 1 $aHawthorne, Nathaniel$d1804-1864

LEADER 00000nz  a2200000o  4500
001 12435
100 1 $aEmerson, Ralph Waldo$d1803-1882
```

Chapter 2. Writing Data

Writing MARC Data

MARC4J provides a `MarcWriter` interface to write MARC data to an output stream. This interface provides two important methods:

`write(Record record)`
> Writes a single `Record` to the output stream.

`close()`
> Closes the writer.

The MARC4J library provides two implementations of `MarcWriter`:

`MarcStreamWriter`
> Writes MARC data in ISO 2709 format.

`MarcXmlWriter`
> Writes MARC data in MARCXML format.

Let's start with writing records in ISO 2709 format. To do this we first need to instantiate a `MarcStreamWriter`:

```
MarcWriter writer = new MarcStreamWriter(System.out);
```

The constructor takes a subclass of `OutputStream` as an argument. You can use `FileOutputStream` to write the output to a file:

```
OutputStream out = new FileOutputStream("output.mrc");
MarcWriter writer = new MarcStreamWriter(out);
```

You can first create a `File` object and use that to create an instance of `FileOutputStream`:

```
File file = new File("output.mrc");
OutputStream out = new FileOutputStream(file);
MarcWriter writer = new MarcStreamWriter(out);
```

To append the output to an existing file, add a boolean argument to the
`FileOutputStream` constructor with the value *true*:

```
File file = new File("output.mrc");
OutputStream out = new FileOutputStream(file, true);
MarcWriter writer = new MarcStreamWriter(out);
```

This can be useful if you want to write records from a number of input files to a single output file.

Let's look at a complete program. Example 2.1, "Write MARC in ISO 2709 Format" updates Example 1.1, "Reading MARC Data" to read the record for *Summerland* in ISO 2709 format and write the same record in ISO 2709 format to standard output.

Example 2.1. Write MARC in ISO 2709 Format

```
import java.io.InputStream;
import java.io.FileInputStream;

import org.marc4j.MarcReader;
import org.marc4j.MarcStreamReader;
import org.marc4j.MarcStreamWriter;
import org.marc4j.MarcWriter;
import org.marc4j.marc.Record;

public class WriteMarcExample {

    public static void main(String args[]) throws Exception {

        InputStream input = new FileInputStream("summerland.mrc");

        MarcReader reader = new MarcStreamReader(input);
        MarcWriter writer = new MarcStreamWriter(System.out);
        while (reader.hasNext()) {
```

```
        Record record = reader.next();
        writer.write(record);
    }
    writer.close();
    }
}
```

Warning

Make sure that you always close the `MarcWriter` using the `close()` method.

Writing MARCXML Data

Instead of using `MarcStreamWriter`, you can use `MarcXmlWriter` to write records in MARCXML format. To do this, you can instantiate a `MarcXmlWriter` using an instance of an `OutputStream` subclass:

```
MarcWriter writer = new MarcXmlWriter(System.out);
```

You can set indent to `true` to format the XML output:

```
MarcWriter writer = new MarcXmlWriter(System.out, true);
```

Example 2.2, "Write MARC in MARCXML Format" reads the record for *Summerland* in ISO 2709 format and writes the same record in MARCXML format to standard output.

Example 2.2. Write MARC in MARCXML Format

```
import java.io.InputStream;
import java.io.FileInputStream;

import org.marc4j.MarcReader;
import org.marc4j.MarcStreamReader;
import org.marc4j.MarcWriter;
```

```
import org.marc4j.MarcXmlWriter;
import org.marc4j.marc.Record;

public class WriteMarcXmlExample {

    public static void main(String args[]) throws Exception {

        InputStream input = new FileInputStream("summerland.mrc");

        MarcReader reader = new MarcStreamReader(input);
        MarcWriter writer = new MarcXmlWriter(System.out, true);

        while (reader.hasNext()) {
            Record record = reader.next();
            writer.write(record);
        }
        writer.close();
    }
}
```

You can also write MARCXML data to MARC in ISO 2709 format by using an instance of
`MarcXmlReader` to read MARCXML data and a `MarcStreamWriter` instance to write
MARC data in ISO 2709 format.

The load time to create a `MarcStreamWriter` or `MarcXmlWriter` is not high, so you
can create an instance to write a single record, for example to output a `Record` object
that was created from scratch:

```
MarcFactory factory = MarcFactory.newInstance();

Record record = factory.newRecord("00000cam a2200000 a 4500");

record.addVariableField(factory.newControlField("001", "12883376"));

DataField dataField = factory.newDataField("245", '1', '0');
dataField.addSubfield(factory.newSubfield('a', "Summerland /"));
dataField.addSubfield(factory.newSubfield('c', "Michael Chabon."));
record.addVariableField(dataField);

MarcWriter writer = new MarcStreamWriter(System.out);
writer.write(record);
writer.close();
```

Performing Character Conversions

When serializing `Record` objects you can perform character conversions. This feature is important when converting MARC data between ISO 2709 and MARCXML formats. Most MARC formats use specific character sets and MARC4J is able to convert some of them to UCS/Unicode and back. Converters are available for the following character encodings:

MARC-8
> Character encoding used by MARC 21 records.

ISO 5426
> Character encoding used by UNIMARC records

ISO 6937
> Character encoding used by UNIMARC records

Using the converters is not difficult, but there are some things to remember. As already stated in Chapter 1, *Reading Data*, MARC4J reads and writes ISO 2709 records as binary data, but data elements in control fields and subfields are converted to `String` values. When Java converts a byte array to a `String` it needs a character encoding. Java can use a default character encoding, but this might not always be the right encoding to use. Therefore both `MarcReader` and `MarWriter` implementations provide you with the ability to set a character encoding when constructing a new instance. The following list summarizes how both `MarcReader` and `MarcWriter` implementations handle character encodings:

`MarcStreamReader`
> By default uses ISO 8859-1 (Latin 1) as 8-bit character set alternative, since encodings like MARC-8 are not supported by Java. In case of MARC 21 data, `MarcStreamReader` tries to detect the encoding from the `Leader` by reading the character coding scheme in the leader using the `getCharCodingScheme()` method. You can override the value when instantiating a `MarcStreamReader`:

```
MarcReader reader = new MarcStreamReader(input, "UTF8");
```

> Please note that `MarcStreamReader` expects a Java encoding name.

`MarcXmlReader`
> By default relies on the underlying XML parser implementation. Normally you would provide the encoding in the XML declaration of the input file:

```
<?xml version="1.0" encoding="UTF-8"?>
```

You can set the character encoding using an `InputSource`, for example:

```
InputStream in = new FileInputStream("summerland.xml");
InputSource is = new InputSource(in);
is.setEncoding("ISO-8859-1");
MarcReader = new MarcXmlReader(is);
```

The `InputSource` uses standard Internet encoding names, rather than Java encoding names. Use for example UTF-8 in stead of UTF8 and ISO-8859-1 instead of ISO8859_1.

`MarcStreamWriter`
By default uses ISO 8859-1 (Latin 1) as 8-bit character set alternative, since encodings like MARC-8 are not supported by Java. You can override the value when instantiating a `MarcStreamWriter`:

```
MarcWriter writer = new MarcStreamWriter(output, "UTF8");
```

Please note that `MarcStreamWriter` expects a Java encoding name.

`MarcXmlWriter`
By default uses UTF-8. You can override the value when instantiating a `MarcXmlWriter`:

```
MarcWriter writer = new MarcXmlWriter(output, "UTF8");
```

Please note that `MarcXmlWriter` expects a Java encoding name. For the encoding in the XML declaration MARC4J relies on the underlying parser.

Check the Java supported encodings for the canonical name to use for a specific encoding. You can find more information in the documentation for the Java 2 Standard Edition. Look for Internationalization in the Guide to Features section.

Let's look at some character conversion examples. Example 2.3, "Convert MARC-8 to UCS/Unicode" reads ISO 2709 records using the default encoding and writes the records in ISO 2709 format performing a MARC-8 to UCS/Unicode conversion. The class `AnselToUnicode` is used to perform the character conversion. This class uses the MARC-8 to Unicode XML mapping file published by the Library of Congress to convert between MARC-8 and UCS/Unicode. The code for the converter was contributed to the MARC4J project by Corey Keith at the time he was working for the Network Development and MARC Standards Office at the Library of Congress.

Example 2.3. Convert MARC-8 to UCS/Unicode

```
import java.io.InputStream;
import java.io.FileInputStream;

import org.marc4j.converter.impl.AnselToUnicode;
import org.marc4j.MarcReader;
import org.marc4j.MarcStreamReader;
import org.marc4j.MarcStreamWriter;
import org.marc4j.MarcWriter;
import org.marc4j.marc.Record;

public class Marc8ToUnicodeExample {

    public static void main(String args[]) throws Exception {

        InputStream input = new FileInputStream("summerland.mrc");

        MarcReader reader = new MarcStreamReader(input);
        MarcWriter writer = new MarcStreamWriter(System.out, "UTF8");

        AnselToUnicode converter = new AnselToUnicode();
        writer.setConverter(converter);

        while (reader.hasNext()) {
            Record record = reader.next();
            writer.write(record);
        }
        writer.close();
    }
}
```

Since `MarcStreamWriter` uses the Latin-1 character encoding by default, the writer is instantiated with the UTF-8 character encoding. When converting MARC records to UTF-8 the leader value for the character coding scheme should also be updated. This is not done by the `MarcStreamWriter` class. You can set the value while iterating over the `Record` objects:

```
while (reader.hasNext()) {
    Record record = reader.next();

    Leader leader = record.getLeader();
    leader.setCharCodingScheme('a');

    writer.write(record);
}
```

Example 2.4, "Convert MARC to MARCXML" converts ISO 2709 records encoded in MARC-8 to MARCXML encoded in UCS/Unicode.

Example 2.4. Convert MARC to MARCXML

```
import java.io.InputStream;
import java.io.FileInputStream;

import java.io.OutputStream;
import java.io.FileOutputStream;

import org.marc4j.converter.impl.AnselToUnicode;
import org.marc4j.MarcReader;
import org.marc4j.MarcStreamReader;
import org.marc4j.MarcStreamWriter;
import org.marc4j.MarcWriter;
import org.marc4j.marc.Record;
import org.marc4j.marc.Leader;

public class MarcToMarcXmlExample {

    public static void main(String args[]) throws Exception {

        InputStream input = new FileInputStream("summerland.mrc");
```

```
OutputStream out = new FileOutputStream("summerland.xml");

MarcReader reader = new MarcStreamReader(input);
MarcWriter writer = new MarcXmlWriter(out, true);

AnselToUnicode converter = new AnselToUnicode();
writer.setConverter(converter);

while (reader.hasNext()) {
    Record record = reader.next();

    Leader leader = record.getLeader();
    leader.setCharCodingScheme('a');

    writer.write(record);
}
writer.close();
    }
}
```

To convert UCS/Unicode back to MARC-8, for example to convert MARCXML back to ISO 2709, you can use the `UnicodeToAnsel` class.

In addition to using a character converter, you can perform Unicode normalization. This is not done by the MARC-8 to UCS/Unicode converter. With Unicode normalization text is transformed into the canonical composed or precomposed form. For example "áฬ'bc" is normalized to "ábc". To perform normalization set Unicode normalization to true:

```
MarcXmlWriter writer = new MarcXmlWriter(out, true);

AnselToUnicode converter = new AnselToUnicode();
writer.setConverter(converter);

writer.setUnicodeNormalization(true);
```

Warning

Please note that it is not guaranteed to work if you try to convert normalized Unicode back to MARC-8 with `UnicodeToAnsel`. The `UnicodeToAnsel` class can only handle non-precomposed Unicode characters.

41

Writing MODS Data

In Chapter 1, *Reading Data* we have seen that you can use a stylesheet to pre-process the input that is given to the `MarcXmlReader`. With `MarcXmlWriter` you can post-process the MARCXML result using an XSLT stylesheet. Example 2.5, "Write MODS Data" converts MARC to MARCXML and transforms the result tree to MODS using the stylesheet provided by the Library of Congress. To do this, you need to add the stylesheet location as an argument when you create the `MarcXmlWriter` instance. Example 2.5, "Write MODS Data" uses an implementation of the `Result` interface to hold the output data:

```
Result result = new StreamResult(System.out);
```

The `Result` interface is part of the JAXP API. This API is covered in more detail in Chapter 3, *MARC4J and JAXP*.

Example 2.5. Write MODS Data

```
import java.io.InputStream;
import java.io.FileOutputStream;

import javax.xml.transform.Result;
import javax.xml.transform.stream.StreamResult;

import org.marc4j.MarcReader;
import org.marc4j.MarcStreamReader;
import org.marc4j.MarcXmlWriter;
import org.marc4j.converter.impl.AnselToUnicode;
import org.marc4j.marc.Record;

public class Marc2ModsExample {

    public static void main(String args[]) throws Exception {

        String stylesheetUrl =
          "http://www.loc.gov/standards/mods/v3/MARC21slim2MODS3.xsl";

        Result result = new StreamResult(System.out);
```

```
InputStream input = new FileInputStream("summerland.mrc");

MarcReader reader = new MarcStreamReader(input);

MarcXmlWriter writer = new MarcXmlWriter(result, stylesheetUri);
writer.setConverter(new AnselToUnicode());

while (reader.hasNext()) {
    Record record = (Record) reader.next();
    writer.write(record);
}
writer.close();
    }
}
```

In addition to the stylesheet which transforms MARCXML data to MODS, the following stylesheets are available from the Library of Congress which transform MARCXML to other formats:

MARCXML to RDF Encoded Simple Dublin Core Stylesheet
    Transforms MARCXML to Dublin Core using the Resource Description Framework (RDF) syntax format. RDF is a language for describing resources in the World Wide Web.

MARCXML to OAI Encoded Simple Dublin Core Stylesheet
    Transforms MARCXML to Dublin Core using the Open Archives Initiative (OAI) syntax format. This syntax is intended for use in the Open Archives Initiative Protocol for Metadata Harvesting.

MARCXML to SRW Encoded Simple Dublin Core Stylesheet
    Transforms MARCXML to Dublin Core using the Search/Retrieve Web Service (SRW) syntax format. SRW is a standard search protocol for Internet search queries. This syntax is intended for use in a searchRetrieve response.

MARCXML to MARC DTD Stylesheet
    Transforms MARCXML to XML conforming to the MARC DTD syntax.

MARC Tagged View
    Transforms MARCXML to HTML to provide a MARC tagged display.

English Tagged View
    Transforms MARCXML to HTML to provide a labelled display.

MARC Bibliographic Validator
    Validates MARCXML against the MARC bibliographic format.

You can find the stylesheets at the Tools & Utilities section of the MARCXML standards page. In Chapter 3, *MARC4J and JAXP* we take a closer look at MARC4J in XML environments.

Chapter 3. MARC4J and JAXP

JAXP Overview

The Java API for XML Processing (JAXP) provides an implementation independent API to process XML with Java. JAXP supports the Simple API for XML (SAX) and Document Object Model (DOM) to parse XML as a stream of events or to build an in-memory object representation. The library also supports XSLT to transform documents to other XML documents, or other text formats. JAXP 1.3 introduced additional packages, including a schema-independent Validation Framework, XPath support, support for W3C XML Schema Data Types and support for XInclude. JAXP 1.3 is part of the J2SE 1.5 release. A stand-alone implementation is available for J2SE 1.3 and 1.4. This chapter focuses on the core classes defined in the following packages:

`javax.xml.parsers`

> Provides processor independent factory classes to obtain a `SAXParser` or `DocumentBuilder` from the underlying XML parser implementation.

`javax.xml.transform`

> Provides processor independent factory classes to obtain an XSLT processor from the underlying implementation. This package is also known as TRAX (Transformation API for XML).

If you do not provide a specific XML parser or XSLT processor implementation, the JAXP implementation will use the default parser that comes with your Java distribution. To use a different implementation, you have to set a system property that points to the parser or processor that should override the default implementation. The easiest way to do this, is to include the system properties in a `jaxp.properties` file located in the `JAVA_HOME/lib` directory. The Xerces parser and Xalan XSLT processor are the default implementations for J2SE 1.5, but J2SE 1.4 by default uses the Crimson XML parser. To use Xerces with J2SE 1.4, you can create a `jaxp.properties` file with the following properties:

```
javax.xml.parsers.SAXParserFactory=
    org.apache.xerces.jaxp.SAXParserFactoryImpl
javax.xml.parsers.DocumentBuilderFactory=
    org.apache.xerces.jaxp.DocumentBuilderFactoryImpl
```

You can also modify your CLASSPATH settings or set the properties at runtime:

```
java -Djavax.xml.parsers.SAXParserFactory=
    org.apache.xerces.jaxp.SAXParserFactoryImpl XercesSerializerExample
```

The XML support in MARC4J is implemented using the interfaces and classes specified in JAXP, so you should be able to use MARC4J with any JAXP compliant parser or processor.

Integration between MARC4J and XML is mainly supported through the Transformation API package. The following interfaces and classes are the most important classes to develop XML applications with MARC4J:

ContentHandler

> The ContentHandler interface is part of SAX (Simple API for XML). Through a ContentHandler a SAX parser reports basic document events like the start and end of elements and character data. When using a SAX based parser, you implement the ContentHandler interface to develop your XML application. This interface is used in the MarcXmlReader class to process the MARCXML input source.

TransformerFactory

> A TransformerFactory instance can be used to create Transformer and Templates objects. A Transformer instance can be used to transform a source document into a result document using an XSLT stylesheet. A Templates object is an in-memory representation of an XSLT stylesheet that can be used to create Transformer objects without the need to read the stylesheet from the file system or the network every time a new Transformer instance is created.

SAXTransformerFactory

> This class extends TransformerFactory to provide SAX specific support. With the SAXTransformerFactory class you can create a TransformerHandler from a Source or Templates object. A TransformerHandler extends the ContentHandler interface. When passed to a MarcXmlWriter instance, the writer will report the MARCXML SAX events to the handler to transform the MARCXML data to a different XML or text format. Instances of TransformerHandler can be chained together to create a pipeline using the setResult(Result) method.

Source

> Implementations of this interface can act as an input source for both XML documents and XSLT stylesheets. JAXP provides three implementations: StreamSource provides an input source from a file or input stream, SAXSource provides an input source from SAX parser events and DOMSource provides an input source from a DOM document.

Result
> Implementations of this interface can act as a holder for a transformation result tree. JAXP provides three implementations: StreamResult can be used to write the result to a file or other output stream, SAXResult can be used to write the result to a ContentHandler and DOMResult can be used to write the result to a DOM document.

Together these interfaces and classes provide a powerful framework to process MARC data in XML environments. In the next sections of this chapter we will look at some examples that illustrate the use of MARC4J with JAXP in XML applications.

Writing To a DOM Document

The Document Object Model (DOM) is a data structure that represents an XML document as a tree of nodes. The basic DOM interface is implemented in the org.w3c.dom package. The interfaces in this package represent elements, attributes, character data, comments, and processing instructions. All of these interfaces are sub-interfaces of the Node interface that provides basic methods to navigate the tree and to add, move, remove, copy or change nodes in the tree. The root of the tree is a Document object that represents a complete XML document.

Using MarcXmlWriter you can write MARCXML to an instance of Document. The DOM document can then be used for further processing in your XML application. To do this, first create an instance of DOMResult:

```
DOMResult result = new DOMResult();
```

You can then use the result to create a MarcXmlWriter:

```
MarcXmlWriter writer = new MarcXmlWriter(result);
```

The writer writes the output to a DOM document that can be retrieved from the result object:

```
Document doc = (Document) result.getNode();
```

Example 3.1, "Writing Output To a DOM Document" shows the complete code. It reads the record for *Summerland* in ISO 2709 format and writes the record as MARCXML to a DOM document.

Example 3.1. Writing Output To a DOM Document

```
import java.io.InputStream;
import java.io.FileInputStream;

import javax.xml.transform.dom.DOMResult;

import org.marc4j.MarcReader;
import org.marc4j.MarcStreamReader;
import org.marc4j.MarcXmlWriter;
import org.marc4j.marc.Record;
import org.w3c.dom.Document;

public class Marc2DomExample {

    public static void main(String args[]) throws Exception {

        InputStream input = new FileInputStream("summerland.mrc");

        MarcReader reader = new MarcStreamReader(input);

        DOMResult result = new DOMResult();

        MarcXmlWriter writer = new MarcXmlWriter(result);

        while (reader.hasNext()) {
            Record record = (Record) reader.next();
            writer.write(record);
        }
        writer.close();

        Document doc = (Document) result.getNode();
    }
}
```

Writing output to a DOM document can be useful when you need to embed the result into a parent document, such as a SOAP (Simple Object Access Protocol) envelope:

```
<?xml version='1.0' ?>
<env:Envelope xmlns:env="http://www.w3.org/2003/05/soap-envelope">
  <env:Body>
    <!-- MARCXML collection -->
  </env:Body>
</env:Envelope>
```

Let's assume that we have a `Document` called `soapEnv`. We can then use the following code to add the `Document` instance, that contains the MARCXML data, to the *env:Body* element of the SOAP envelope:

```
// the object containing the MARCXML data
Document doc = (Document) result.getNode();

// import the node in the SOAP document
Node marcxml = soapEnv.importNode(doc.getDocumentElement(), true);

// get the SOAP body element
Element soapBody = (Element)
    soapEnv.getElementsByTagName("env:Body").item(0);

// append the node containing the MARCXML data
// to the SOAP Body element
soapBody.appendChild(marcxml);
```

You can post-process the MARCXML data before writing the result to a DOM document using an XSLT stylesheet. The following listing transforms MARC records to MODS and writes the MODS data to a DOM document:

```
String stylesheetUrl =
    "http://www.loc.gov/standards/mods/v3/MARC21slim2MODS3.xsl";
Source stylesheet = new StreamSource(stylesheetUrl);

DOMResult result = new DOMResult();
MarcXmlWriter writer = new MarcXmlWriter(result, stylesheet);
```

```
while (reader.hasNext()) {
    Record record = (Record) reader.next();
    writer.write(record);
}
writer.close();

Document doc = (Document) result.getNode();
```

Formatting Output with Xerces

Example 3.1, "Writing Output To a DOM Document" demonstrated that you can write the output of MarcXmlWriter to an implementation of the Result interface, in this case DOMResult. My favorite implementation of the Result interface is the SAXResult class. The MarcXmlWriter class provides very basic formatting options. If you need more advanced formatting, you can use a SAXResult to hold a ContentHandler derived from a dedicated XML serializer. Example 3.2, "Formatting Output with the Xerces Serializer" uses the Xerces XMLSerializer class to write MARC records to XML. The program also converts characters from MARC-8 to UCS/Unicode and performs Unicode normalization. The XMLSerializer class provides a lot of formatting options and it knows how to handle namespaces reported by the SAX startPrefixMapping() and endPrefixMapping() events. Using the serializer is simple. The first step is to configure the output format with the serialization options you want:

```
OutputFormat format = new OutputFormat("xml", "UTF-8", true);
```

The OutputFormat class provides all kinds of formatting options including indentation and the maximum line length. In this case the output method is *xml*, the output encoding is *UTF-8* and indentation is set to true. The object is used to create an instance of XMLSerializer. In this example the output is written to standard output:

```
XMLSerializer serializer = new XMLSerializer(System.out, format);
```

To be able to register the serializer, you need to wrap the instance in a SAXResult:

```
Result result = new SAXResult(serializer.asContentHandler());
```

You can then use the `SAXResult` to create an instance of `MarcXmlWriter`. Example 3.2, "Formatting Output with the Xerces Serializer" shows the complete code.

Example 3.2. Formatting Output with the Xerces Serializer

```
import java.io.InputStream;
import java.io.FileInputStream;

import javax.xml.transform.Result;
import javax.xml.transform.sax.SAXResult;

import org.apache.xml.serialize.OutputFormat;
import org.apache.xml.serialize.XMLSerializer;
import org.marc4j.MarcReader;
import org.marc4j.MarcStreamReader;
import org.marc4j.MarcXmlWriter;
import org.marc4j.converter.impl.AnselToUnicode;
import org.marc4j.marc.Record;
import org.marc4j.marc.Leader;

public class XercesSerializerExample {

    public static void main(String args[]) throws Exception {

        InputStream input = new FileInputStream("summerland.mrc");

        MarcReader reader = new MarcStreamReader(input);

        // configure the output format
        OutputFormat format = new OutputFormat("xml", "UTF-8", true);

        // create the serializer
        XMLSerializer serializer = new XMLSerializer(System.out, format);

        // create the result
        Result result = new SAXResult(serializer.asContentHandler());

        MarcXmlWriter writer = new MarcXmlWriter(result);
```

```
writer.setConverter(new AnselToUnicode());
writer.setUnicodeNormalization(true);

while  reader.hasNext() {
    Record record = reader.next();

    Leader leader = record.getLeader();
    leader.setCharCodingScheme('a');

    writer.write(record);
}
writer.close();

    }
}
```

Tip

Since `MarcXmlWriter` only provides limited formatting options, it is recommended to always use a dedicated XML serializer like Xerces `XMLSerializer`.

Compiling Stylesheets

If you need to transform input from many files, you can instantiate `MarcXmlReader` with a compiled stylesheet to speed up the process. The XSLT processor will then use the in-memory stylesheet data rather than re-parse the entire stylesheet for every file. A compiled stylesheet is represented by the `Templates` class. The `MarcXmlReader` class provides a constructor that takes a `TransformerHandler` as an argument. A `TransformerHandler` listens for SAX parse events and transforms them to a `Result`. For each transformation we need a new instance of `TransformerHandler`. You can obtain the handler from a `Templates` object containing the in-memory stylesheet representation. To demonstrate the use of a compiled stylesheet, we create a program that reads files containing MODS data from a given directory on the file system. For each file it transforms the MODS records to MARCXML and writes each record in tagged display format to standard output.

The first step is to create an instance of `TransformerFactory`:

```
TransformerFactory tf = TransformerFactory.newInstance();
```

You can then create a `Templates` object to hold the in-memory stylesheet representation:

```
Source stylesheet = new StreamSource(
    "http://www.loc.gov/standards/marcxml/xslt/MODS2MARC21slim.xsl");

Templates templates = tf.newTemplates(stylesheet);
```

To read files from the file system, a filter is used to limit the list to XML files:

```
File dir = new File(inputDir);

FilenameFilter filter = new FilenameFilter() {
    public boolean accept(File dir, String name) {
        return name.endsWith(".xml");
    }
};

File[] files = dir.listFiles(filter);
```

To create the `TransformerHandler`, you first need to cast the `TransformerFactory` to a `SAXTransformerFactory`:

```
SAXTransformerFactory stf = ((SAXTransformerFactory) tf);
```

You can then read files from the file list and process each file using `MarcXmlReader`:

```
for (int i = 0; i < files.length; i++) {

    TransformerHandler handler = stf.newTransformerHandler(templates);

    InputStream input = new FileInputStream(files[i]);

    MarcReader reader = new MarcXmlReader(input, handler);

    while (reader.hasNext()) {
        Record record = reader.next();
```

```
        System.out.println(record.toString());
    }

}
```

Example 3.3, "Reading MODS from Multiple Files" shows the complete code.

Example 3.3. Reading MODS from Multiple Files

```
import java.io File;
import java.io FileInputStream;
import java.io FilenameFilter;
import java.io InputStream;

import javax.xml.transform.Source;
import javax.xml.transform.Templates;
import javax.xml.transform.TransformerFactory;
import javax.xml.transform.sax.SAXResult;
import javax.xml.transform.sax.SAXSource;
import javax.xml.transform.sax.SAXTransformerFactory;
import javax.xml.transform.sax.TransformerHandler;
import javax.xml.transform.stream.StreamSource;

import org.marc4j.MarcReader;
import org.marc4j.MarcXmlReader;
import org.marc4j.marc.Record;

public class TemplatesExample {

    public static void main(String args[]) throws Exception {
        if (args.length != 1))
            throw new Exception("Usage: TemplatesExample <dir>")

        String inputDir = args[0];

        TransformerFactory tf = TransformerFactory.newInstance();

        if (tf.getFeature(SAXSource.FEATURE)
                && tf.getFeature(SAXResult.FEATURE)) {

            // create a stylesheet source
```

```
        Source stylesheet = new StreamSource(
"http://www.loc.gov/standards/marcxml/xslt/MODS2MARC21slim.xsl");

        // create an in-memory stylesheet representation
        Templates templates = tf.newTemplates(stylesheet);

        File dir = new File(inputDir);

        // create a filter to include only .xml files
        FilenameFilter filter = new FilenameFilter() {
            public boolean accept(File dir, String name) {
                return name.endsWith(".xml");
            }
        };

        // list all files
        File[] files = dir.listFiles(filter);

        // cast the transformer handler to a sax transformer handler
        SAXTransformerFactory stf = ((SAXTransformerFactory) tf);

        // iterate over all files
        for (int i = 0; i < files.length; i++) {

            // create a transformer handler from the template
            TransformerHandler handler = stf
                    .newTransformerHandler(templates);

            // create the input stream
            InputStream input = new FileInputStream(files[i]);

            // parse the input stream and write each record
            MarcReader reader = new MarcXmlReader(input, handler);
            while (reader.hasNext()) {
                Record record = reader.next();
                System.out.println(record.toString());
            }
        }
    }
}


}
```

Chaining Stylesheets

You can chain `TransformerHandler` instances together to create a pipeline that sends the XML data through a sequence of stages. For each stylesheet in the chain a `TransformerHandler` is created. In Example 3.4, "Stylesheet Chain" the XML data goes through the following three stages:

1. The first handler receives SAX events from the `MarcXmlWriter` that converts the ISO 2709 input to MARCXML. It then transforms the MARCXML data to MODS and sends the result to the second handler.

2. The second handler transforms the SAX events received from the first handler back to MARCXML. Let's assume that we want to check if there is any loss of data between the transformations.

3. The third handler receives the MARCXML data from the second handler and writes the MARCXML data to a tagged display format in HTML using the *MARC21slim2HTML.xsl* stylesheet.

First a `TransformerHandler` is created for each stylesheet by obtaining an instance from the `SAXTransformerFactory`. The stylesheets are then chained together using the `setResult()` method so that each transformation step passes its output to the next step:

```
tHandler1.setResult(new SAXResult(tHandler2));
tHandler2.setResult(new SAXResult(tHandler3));
```

The third and final transformation step writes the result to the file `output.html`:

```
OutputStream out = new FileOutputStream("output.html");
tHandler3.setResult(new StreamResult(out));
```

The `TransformerHandler` that performs the first transformation step is wrapped in a `SAXResult` to create the instance of `MarcXmlWriter`. Example 3.4, "Stylesheet Chain" shows the complete code for the stylesheet chain program.

Example 3.4. Stylesheet Chain

```java
import java.io.InputStream;
import java.io.FileInputStream;
import java.io.OutputStream;
import java.io.FileOutputStream;

import javax.xml.transform.Result;
import javax.xml.transform.TransformerFactory;
import javax.xml.transform.sax.SAXResult;
import javax.xml.transform.sax.SAXSource;
import javax.xml.transform.sax.SAXTransformerFactory;
import javax.xml.transform.sax.TransformerHandler;
import javax.xml.transform.stream.StreamResult;
import javax.xml.transform.stream.StreamSource;

import org.marc4j.MarcReader;
import org.marc4j.MarcStreamReader;
import org.marc4j.MarcWriter;
import org.marc4j.MarcXmlWriter;
import org.marc4j.marc.Record;

public class StylesheetChainExample {

    public static void main(String args[]) throws Exception {

        TransformerFactory tf = TransformerFactory.newInstance();

        if (tf.getFeature(SAXSource.FEATURE)
                && tf.getFeature(SAXResult.FEATURE)) {

            // cast the transformer handler to a sax transformer handler
            SAXTransformerFactory stf = ((SAXTransformerFactory) tf);

            // create a TransformerHandler for each stylesheet.
            TransformerHandler tHandler1 = stf
                .newTransformerHandler(new StreamSource(
        "http://www.loc.gov/standards/mods/v3/MARC21slim2MODS3.xsl"));

            TransformerHandler tHandler2 = stf
                .newTransformerHandler(new StreamSource(
        "http://www.loc.gov/standards/marcxml/xslt/MODS2MARC21slim.xsl"));
```

```
        TransformerHandler tHandler3 = stf
            .newTransformerHandler(new StreamSource(
   "http://www.loc.gov/standards/marcxml/xslt/MARC21slim2HTML.xsl"));

        // chain the transformer handlers
        tHandler1.setResult(new SAXResult(tHandler2));
        tHandler2.setResult(new SAXResult(tHandler3));

        // create an output stream
        OutputStream out = new FileOutputStream("output.html");
        tHandler3.setResult(new StreamResult(out));

        // create a SAXResult with the first handler
        Result result = new SAXResult(tHandler1);

        // create the input stream
        InputStream input = new FileInputStream("summerland.mrc");

        // parse the input
        MarcReader reader = new MarcStreamReader(input);
        MarcWriter writer = new MarcXmlWriter(result);
        while (reader.hasNext()) {
            Record record = reader.next();
            writer.write(record);
        }
        writer.close();

        out.close();
    }
  }
}
```

When you compile and run this program, it will write each record in tagged display format to the file output.html. Figure 3.1, "Stylesheet Chain Output" shows the output for the *Summerland* record used in Example 3.4, "Stylesheet Chain".

Figure 3.1. Stylesheet Chain Output

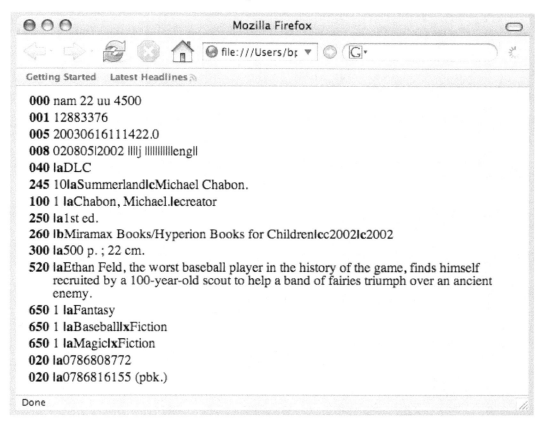

Within the browser window:

```
000 nam 22 uu 4500
001 12883376
005 20030616111422.0
008 020805l2002 llllj lllllllllllengll
040 laDLC
245 10laSummerlandlcMichael Chabon.
100 1 laChabon, Michael.lecreator
250 la1st ed.
260 lbMiramax Books/Hyperion Books for Childrenlcc2002lc2002
300 la500 p. ; 22 cm.
520 laEthan Feld, the worst baseball player in the history of the game, finds himself
    recruited by a 100-year-old scout to help a band of fairies triumph over an ancient
    enemy.
650 1 laFantasy
650 1 laBaseballlxFiction
650 1 laMagiclxFiction
020 la0786808772
020 la0786816155 (pbk.)
```

Creating a Dublin Core Writer

If you do not want to rely on a stylesheet to post-process MARCXML into the desired XML format, you can implement your own `MarcWriter`. One approach to do this, is to implement a `ContentHandler` that produces SAX events. You can then serialize the events to XML using a serializer that consumes the SAX events. The benefit is that your writer will be very fast and will have a low memory consumption. The disadvantage of this approach is that it requires some low level SAX programming. Using a `ContentHandler` to create XML is not difficult, but it can be a challenge to create code that is nice and clean. These are the methods a `ContentHandler` provides:

```
characters(char[] ch, int start, int length)
```
Receive notification of character data.

```
endDocument()
```
Receive notification of the end of a document.

```
endElement(String uri, String localName, String qName)
```
Receive notification of the end of an element.

```
endPrefixMapping(String prefix)
```
End the scope of a prefix-URI mapping.

```
ignorableWhitespace(char[] ch, int start, int length)
```
Receive notification of ignorable whitespace in element content.

```
processingInstruction(String target, String data)
```
Receive notification of a processing instruction.

```
setDocumentLocator(Locator locator)
```
Receive an object for locating the origin of SAX document events.

```
skippedEntity(String name)
```
Receive notification of a skipped entity.

```
startDocument()
```
Receive notification of the beginning of a document.

```
startElement(String uri, String localName, String qName,
Attributes atts)
```
Receive notification of the beginning of an element.

```
startPrefixMapping(String prefix, String uri)
```
Begin the scope of a prefix-URI Namespace mapping.

Although SAX was designed to read XML data, you can also use these methods to create XML. To do this you only need an implementation of ContentHandler that is able to serialize XML, like the Xerces XMLSerializer used in Example 3.2, "Formatting Output with the Xerces Serializer". Example 3.5, "Output Dublin Core Title Element" shows a simple program that outputs a Dublin Core *title* element.

Example 3.5. Output Dublin Core Title Element

```
import org.apache.xml.serialize.XMLSerializer;
import org.xml.sax.Attributes;
import org.xml.sax.ContentHandler;
import org.xml.sax.helpers.AttributesImpl;

public class SaxProducerExample {

    public static final String DC_NS =
        "http://purl.org/dc/elements/1.1/";

    public static final Attributes atts = new AttributesImpl();

    public static void main(String args[]) throws Exception {

        // create a serializer
        XMLSerializer serializer = new XMLSerializer(System.out, null);
        ContentHandler ch = serializer.asContentHandler();

        // start the document
        ch.startDocument();
        ch.startPrefixMapping("", DC_NS);

        // write the title element
        ch.startElement(DC_NS, "title", "title", atts);
        char[] data = "Summerland".toCharArray();
        ch.characters(data, 0, data.length);
        ch.endElement(DC_NS, "title", "title");

        // end the document
        ch.endPrefixMapping("");
        ch.endDocument();
    }

}
```

When you compile and run this program, it will write the following XML document to standard output:

```
<?xml version="1.0"?>
<title xmlns="http://purl.org/dc/elements/1.1/">Summerland</title>
```

You can use this approach to create a `MarcWriter` implementation that reports SAX events to a `ContentHandler` implementation:

```
public class MarcDublinCoreWriter implements MarcWriter {

    private ContentHandler ch;

    public MarcDublinCoreWriter(ContentHandler ch) {
        this.ch = ch;
        // start document
    }

    public void write(Record record) {
        // create Dublin Core record
    }

    public void close() {
        // end document
    }

}
```

Example 3.6, "Dublin Core Writer" shows the code for a `MarcWriter` implementation that creates Dublin Core. It is not a full implementation of the MARC 21 to Dublin Core crosswalk: it writes the *creator*, *title* and *subject* elements to the `ContentHandler`.

The two `getDataElements()` methods are helper methods to concatenate the given subfield data elements and return the result as a character array. Since MARC is richer in data than Dublin Core, in some cases multiple MARC data elements are mapped to a single Dublin Core element. The method iterates over a character array containing subfield codes. If there is a match, the data element is added to the `StringBuffer` preceded by a space. The data is converted before it is returned if a registered character converter is present.

Example 3.6. Dublin Core Writer

```java
import java.util.Iterator;
import java.util.List;

import org.marc4j.MarcException;
import org.marc4j.MarcWriter;
import org.marc4j.converter.CharConverter;
import org.marc4j.marc.DataField;
import org.marc4j.marc.Record;
import org.marc4j.marc.Subfield;
import org.xml.sax.Attributes;
import org.xml.sax.ContentHandler;
import org.xml.sax.SAXException;
import org.xml.sax.helpers.AttributesImpl;

public class DublinCoreWriter implements MarcWriter {

    public static final String RDF_NS =
        "http://www.w3.org/1999/02/22-rdf-syntax-ns#";

    public static final String DC_NS =
        "http://purl.org/dc/elements/1.1/";

    public static final Attributes atts = new AttributesImpl();

    private ContentHandler ch;

    private CharConverter converter = null;

    public DublinCoreWriter(ContentHandler ch) {
        this.ch = ch;
        try {
            ch.startDocument();
            ch.startPrefixMapping("rdf", RDF_NS);
            ch.startPrefixMapping("dc", DC_NS);
            ch.startElement(RDF_NS, "Description", "rdf:Description",
                atts);
        } catch (SAXException e) {
            throw new MarcException(e.getMessage(), e);
        }
    }
```

```
public void close() {
    try {
        ch.endElement(RDF_NS, "Description", "rdf:Description");
        ch.endPrefixMapping("dc");
        ch.endPrefixMapping("rdf");
        ch.endDocument();
    } catch (SAXException e) {
        throw new MarcException(e.getMessage(), e);
    }

}

public CharConverter getConverter() {
    return converter;
}

public void setConverter(CharConverter converter) {
    this.converter = converter;
}

public void write(Record record) {
    DataField field;
    char[] data;

    try {
        field = (DataField) record.getVariableField("100");
        if (field != null) {
            data = getDataElements(field);
            ch.startElement(DC_NS, "creator", "dc:creator", atts);
            ch.characters(data, 0, data.length);
            ch.endElement(DC_NS, "creator", "dc:creator");
        }

        field = (DataField) record.getVariableField("245");
        if (field != null) {
            data = getDataElements(field, "abfghk");
            ch.startElement(DC_NS, "title", "dc:title", atts);
            ch.characters(data, 0, data.length);
            ch.endElement(DC_NS, "title", "dc:title");
        }

        String[] subjects = { "600", "610", "611", "630", "650" };
        List list = record.getVariableFields(subjects);
        Iterator i = list.iterator();
```

```
        while (i.hasNext()) {
            field = (DataField) i.next();
            data = getDataElements(field);
            ch.startElement(DC_NS, "subject", "dc:subject", atts);
            ch.characters(data, 0, data.length);
            ch.endElement(DC_NS, "subject", "dc:subject");
        }

    } catch (SAXException e) {
        throw new MarcException(e.getMessage(), e);
    }

}

private char[] getDataElements(DataField field) {
    return getDataElements(field, null);
}

private char[] getDataElements(DataField field, String codeString) {
    StringBuffer sb = new StringBuffer();

    char[] codes = "abcdefghijklmnopqrstuvwxyz".toCharArray();

    if (codeString != null)
        codes = codeString.toCharArray();

    for (int i = 0; i < codes.length; i++) {
        Subfield sf = field.getSubfield(codes[i]);
        if (sf != null) {
            if (i > 1)
                sb.append(" ");
            sb.append(sf.getData());
        }
    }
    if (converter == null)
        return sb.toString().toCharArray();
    else {
        String data = converter.convert(sb.toString());
        return data.toCharArray();
    }
}

}
```

Example 3.7, "Driver for DublinCoreWriter" provides a driver to demonstrate the use of `DublinCoreWriter` in a program. It reads the record for *Summerland* and writes the record as a Dublin Core document to standard output using the Xerces `XMLSerializer`.

Example 3.7. Driver for DublinCoreWriter

```java
import java.io.InputStream;
import java.io.FileInputStream;

import org.apache.xml.serialize.OutputFormat;
import org.apache.xml.serialize.XMLSerializer;
import org.marc4j.MarcReader;
import org.marc4j.MarcStreamReader;
import org.marc4j.MarcWriter;
import org.marc4j.marc.Record;
import org.xml.sax.ContentHandler;

public class DublinCoreWriterExample {

    public static void main(String args[]) throws Exception {

        InputStream input = new FileInputStream("summerland.mrc");

        MarcReader reader = new MarcStreamReader(in);

        OutputFormat format = new OutputFormat("xml", "UTF-8", true);
        XMLSerializer serializer = new XMLSerializer(System.out, format);
        ContentHandler ch = serializer.asContentHandler();

        MarcWriter writer = new DublinCoreWriter(ch);
        while (reader.hasNext()) {
            Record record = (Record) reader.next();
            writer.write(record);
        }
        writer.close();

    }

}
```

When you compile and run this program, it will write the following document to standard output:

```
<?xml version="1.0" encoding="UTF-8"?>
<rdf:Description
    xmlns:rdf="http://www.w3.org/1999/02/22-rdf-syntax-ns#"
    xmlns:dc="http://purl.org/dc/elements/1.1/">
  <dc:creator>Chabon, Michael.</dc:creator>
  <dc:title>Summerland /</dc:title>
  <dc:subject>Fantasy.</dc:subject>
  <dc:subject>Baseball Fiction.</dc:subject>
  <dc:subject>Magic Fiction.</dc:subject>
</rdf:Description>
```

Implementing a `MarcWriter` to serialize `Record` objects to XML requires some low level SAX programming, but if you have high performance demands and require low memory consumption, you might want to consider this approach.

Chapter 4. Indexing with Lucene

Introduction

In this chapter we add text indexing and searching to a MARC4J application using Apache Lucene. Lucene is a high-performance text search engine library written in Java. Like MARC4J, Lucene is a low-level API, but in order to start using it, you only need to know how to use a few of its classes. MARC4J provides a `MarcWriter` implementation called `MarcIndexWriter` to create a Lucene index from `Record` objects, making indexing MARC data a breeze. When you create an index using `MarcIndexWriter`, you add documents to an index using the `write(Record)` method specified in the `MarcWriter` interface.

Installation

To use Lucene with MARC4J, you need to download a binary release of Lucene and a library containing the `MarcIndexWriter`. This package is not bundled with MARC4J, but you can find it at the Documents & Files section of the MARC4J project at http://marc4j.tigris.org. Look for *marc4j-lucene-0.1.zip* or *marc4j-lucene-0.1.tar.gz*. You can download a binary release of Lucene at the website for the Apache Lucene project. The MARC4J Lucene library uses Lucene version 2.0.0, so make sure you download this version or a later release. Add `lucene-core-2.0.0.jar`, `marc4j-lucene.jar`, `marc4j.jar` and `commons-logging-1.1.jar` to your CLASSPATH environment variable. The `marc4j-lucene.jar` and `commons-logging-1.1.jar` packages are included in the download for the MARC4J Lucene API.

Index Configuration

The core classes for indexing text with Lucene are `IndexWriter`, `Directory`, `Analyzer`, `Document`, and `Field`. `IndexWriter` is used to create a new index and to add `Documents` to an existing index. Before text is indexed, it is passed through an `Analyzer` when the field is flagged as tokenized. Analyzers extract tokens out of text to be indexed, and ignore the rest. Lucene comes with a number of `Analyzer` implementations, including analyzers for different languages. The examples in this book all use the `StandardAnalyzer`. It is considered the most generally useful analyzer. By default this class uses an English stop-word list that can be overridden when creating an instance. `StandardAnalyzer` provides a sophisticated lexical analyzer that keeps together tokens like e-mail adresses, host names or words with an interior apostrophe.

An index consists of a collection of documents, and each document consists of one or more fields. Each field has a name and a value. A field *title* can for example hold the title proper. Fields are repeatable, so you can have multiple fields with the same name. The `Directory` class is an abstract class that represents the location of a Lucene index. Lucene provides a number of `Directory` implementations, including `FSDirectory`, to store an index in a directory on the file system and `RAMDirectory` to hold a fast in-memory index.

To enable `MarcIndexWriter` to index your MARC records, you need to provide a configuration file with information about the way your MARC data should be indexed by Lucene. If you do not provide a configuration file, `MarcIndexWriter` will use the one that is included in the library. The default configuration is based on the MARC 21 to Dublin Core crosswalk. Table 4.1, "Default Indexing Schema" provides a mapping of the fields and the data elements that are indexed.

Table 4.1. Default Indexing Schema

Lucene Field	MARC Data Elements
dc.type	Leader character position 6 and tag 655 subfield code a.
dc.format	Tag 856 subfield code q.
dc.language	Tag 008 character positions 35-37.
dc.creator	Tags 100, 110, 111, 700, 710, 711, 720.
dc.title	Tag 245.
dc.publisher	Tag 260 subfield code a and b.
dc.date	Tag 260 subfield code c.
dc.description	Tags 500, 504, 505, 520, 521.
dc.subject	Tags 600, 610, 611, 630, 650, 653.
dc.coverage	Tag 651.
dc.relation	Tags 530, 760, 762, 765, 767, 770, 772-777, 780, 785-787.
dc.identifier	Tag 020 subfield code a and tag 856 subfield code u.
dc.rights	Tag 506 subfield code s, tag 540 subfield code a.
controlnumber	Tag 001.
record	Contains the ISO 2709 data as a compressed byte stream.

The examples in this chapter are taken from this schema. Creating a configuration file is simple. We start with the basic XML document:

```
<?xml version="1.0" encoding="UTF-8"?>
<!DOCTYPE document PUBLIC "-//MARC4J//DTD Indexing Schema//EN"
    "http://marc4j.org/dtd/indexing-schema.dtd">
<document>
  <!-- add fields here -->
</document>
```

It is important to include the reference to the XML DTD (Document Type Definition) to declare that the configuration document conforms to the MARC4J Indexing Schema DTD. The `MarcIndexWriter` instance validates the XML configuration against this schema and an error will be thrown if the program is unable to locate it. The `MarcIndexWriter` class uses the declaration as a key to find the schema file in the resource bundle. As you can see the root element is *document*, corresponding to a document in Lucene. The next step is to add an index field to the configuration document:

```
<?xml version="1.0" encoding="UTF-8"?>
<!DOCTYPE document PUBLIC "-//MARC4J//DTD Indexing Schema//EN"
    "http://marc4j.org/dtd/indexing-schema.dtd">
<document>
  <field name="controlnumber" index="untokenized" store="yes">
    <controlfield tag="001"/>
  </field>
</document>
```

This document has a single field named *controlnumber* containing the control number (tag 001) as a value. The control number is added as an untokenized value to the index. This means that it is not tokenized by an analyzer. The control number is stored so it can be used as a reference to the MARC record.

In this example the whole control field value is added, but it is also possible to specify a data element at particular character positions. The following field element specifies a field *dc.language* with the MARC language code taken from character positions 35-37 of the fixed-length data elements (tag 008).

```
<field name="dc.language" index="untokenized" store="no">
  <controlfield tag="008" start="35" end="37"/>
</field>
```

As shown in the *controlnumber* field, the *start* and *end* attributes are not required. You can use the *start* attribute without an *end* attribute to specify a single character data element. Leader values are added in a similar way using a *leader* element. The following listing adds a field *dc.type* containing the leader value for the type of record:

```
<field name="dc.type" index="untokenized" store="no">
  <leader start="6"/>
</field>
```

You can add an *end* attribute for leader values consisting of more than one character, although it might not be very useful.

A text index would not be of much use without data fields containing the actual bibliographic information. The following *field* element specifies a *dc.title* field with the title and remainder of title subfields:

```
<field name="dc.title" index="tokenized" store="no">
  <datafield tag="245">
    <subfield>a</subfield>
    <subfield>b</subfield>
  </datafield>
</field>
```

The title and remainder of title subfields are added as tokenized values. This means that the data elements are passed through the StandardAnalyzer before text is added to the index.

You are not required to add a separate *subfield* element for each subfield code. The following short notation is also valid:

```
<field name="dc.title" index="tokenized" store="no">
  <datafield tag="245">
    <subfield>ab</subfield>
```

```
    </datafield>
  </field>
```

A single index field can contain multiple data elements. To create a field named *dc.subject* containing subject access fields, you can do the following:

```
<field name="dc.subject" index="tokenized" store="no">
  <datafield tag="600">
    <subfield>abcdefghjklmnopqrstu4vxyz</subfield>
  </datafield>
  <datafield tag="610">
    <subfield>abcdefghklmnoprstu4vxyz</subfield>
  </datafield>
  <datafield tag="611">
    <subfield>acdefghklnpqstu4vxyz</subfield>
   </datafield>
  <datafield tag="630">
    <subfield>adfghklmnoprstvxyz</subfield>
  </datafield>
  <datafield tag="650">
    <subfield>aevxyz</subfield>
  </datafield>
  <datafield tag="653">
    <subfield>a</subfield>
   </datafield>
</field>
```

You can also mix leader values, control fields and data fields within a single index field. The listing below specifies a field named *dc.date* with the date from the fixed-length data elements and the date of publication as values:

```
<field name="dc.date" index="tokenized" store="no">
  <controlfield tag="008" start="7" end="10"/>
  <datafield tag="260">
    <subfield>c</subfield>
  </datafield>
</field>
```

In addition to the MARC data elements, it is possible to configure `MarcIndexWriter` to store the full MARC record in Lucene as a byte array:

```
<field name="record" index="no" store="compress">
  <record/>
</field>
```

This adds a field named *record* to the document with a compressed byte stream containing the full MARC record. In this case the *index* attribute is ignored since it is not possible to index a binary field in Lucene.

Creating an Index

Example 4.1, "Creating an Index" shows a command-line program that creates an index based on the default index configuration. It takes two arguments: the path where Lucene should create the index and the input file.

Example 4.1. Creating an Index

```java
import java.io.File;
import java.io.FileInputStream;
import java.io.InputStream;

import org.apache.lucene.analysis.Analyzer;
import org.apache.lucene.analysis.standard.StandardAnalyzer;
import org.apache.lucene.index.IndexWriter;
import org.marc4j.MarcReader;
import org.marc4j.MarcStreamReader;
import org.marc4j.lucene.MarcIndexWriter;
import org.marc4j.marc.Record;

public class CreateIndexSample {

    public static void main(String args[]) throws Exception {
        if (args.length != 2)
            throw new Exception("Usage: CreateIndexSample " +
                "<index> <input>");

        File indexDir = new File(args[0]);
```

```
        File inputFile = new File(args[1]);

        InputStream in = new FileInputStream(inputFile);

        // create a Lucene index writer
        Analyzer analyzer = new StandardAnalyzer();
        IndexWriter indexWriter = new IndexWriter(indexDir,
                analyzer, true);

        // create the index writer for record objects
        MarcIndexWriter writer = new MarcIndexWriter(indexWriter);

        // read records and add them to the index
        MarcReader reader = new MarcStreamReader(in, "UTF8");
        while (reader.hasNext()) {
            Record record = reader.next();
            writer.write(record);
        }
        System.out.println("Documents: " + indexWriter.docCount());

        // close the index writer
        writer.close();
    }

}
```

The `IndexWriter` uses the path to the index directory as the index location. The `StandardAnalyzer` is used to tokenize the fields. The boolean value *true* instructs `IndexWriter` to create the index, or overwrite an existing one. The `IndexWriter` object is used by `MarcIndexWriter` to add documents to the index. To index data using a custom index configuration, the `MarcIndexWriter` class provides two additional constructors that take a byte stream or a system identifier as an argument.

Example 4.1, "Creating an Index" uses `MarcStreamReader` to read records from the input stream in ISO 2709 format, but you can also use `MarcXmlReader` to add MARCXML data to the index.

Andrzej Bialecki created a tool called Luke that provides an index browser for Lucene. It is a very helpful tool to browse the structure of a Lucene index or to perform ad-hoc queries. You can launch Luke via Java Web Start from the Luke web site. Figure 4.1, "Luke Overview Tab" shows the Overview tab. It displays the index name, number of fields, documents and terms. It also allows you to browse fields and terms.

Figure 4.1. Luke Overview Tab

Searching

Now that you have created the index, you can start using it to search. Example 4.2, "Searching the Index" creates an instance of `IndexSearcher` using the index location provided as an argument. It then searches the index for records that have a title with value *Summerland*.

Example 4.2. Searching the Index

```
import java.io.File;

import org.apache.lucene.analysis.Analyzer;
```

```
import org.apache.lucene.analysis.standard.StandardAnalyzer;
import org.apache.lucene.queryParser.QueryParser;
import org.apache.lucene.search.Hits;
import org.apache.lucene.search.IndexSearcher;
import org.apache.lucene.search.Query;
import org.apache.lucene.store.Directory;
import org.apache.lucene.store.FSDirectory;

public class SearchIndexSample {

    public static void main(String args[]) throws Exception {
        if (args.length != 1)
            throw new Exception("Usage: SearchIndexSample <index>");

        File indexDir = new File(args[0]);

        // create a Lucene index searcher
        Directory dir = FSDirectory.getDirectory(indexDir, false);
        IndexSearcher searcher = new IndexSearcher(dir);

        // search by title
        Analyzer analyzer = new StandardAnalyzer();
        QueryParser parser = new QueryParser("title", analyzer);
        Query q = parser.parse("Summerland");
        Hits hits = searcher.search(q);
        System.out.println("Hits: " + hits.length());
    }

}
```

As you can see in the imports, searching the index does not require any MARC4J classes. All that you need to know is the location of the index that has been created using the `MarcIndexWriter`. It is used to create a `Directory` instance that is required to instantiate the `IndexSearcher` object:

```
File indexDir = new File(args[0]);

// create a Lucene index searcher
Directory dir = FSDirectory.getDirectory(indexDir, false);
IndexSearcher searcher = new IndexSearcher(dir);
```

The core classes to execute queries are `TermQuery`, `Term`, `QueryParser`, `Query` and `Hits`. When searching tokenized fields, it is important to provide the same analyzer that has been used to create the index:

```
Analyzer analyzer = new StandardAnalyzer();
QueryParser parser = new QueryParser("title", analyzer);
Query q = parser.parse("Summerland");
Hits hits = searcher.search(q);
```

For untokenized fields, like the *controlnumber* field, you can add the field directly to a query:

```
TermQuery q = new TermQuery(new Term("controlnumber", "11939876"));
Hits hits = searcher.search(q);
```

Once you have an instance of `Hits`, you can retrieve the Lucene documents. The index is created using the default configuration. Since it stores the whole record as a byte array, you can retrieve the full MARC record in ISO 2709 format and unmarshal it to a `Record` object. To do this, you first retrieve the `Document` instance from the `Hits` object:

```
Document doc = hits.doc(i);
```

You can then get the binary value for the *record* field using the `getBinaryValue(String)` method:

```
byte[] bytes = doc.getBinaryValue("record");
```

This method returns the record as a byte stream. You can unmarshal the byte stream using the `RecordUtils` class provided by the MARC4J Lucene library:

```
Record record = RecordUtils.unmarshal(bytes);
```

In Example 4.3, "Searching the Index and Retrieving Records" the retrieval of the record object is added to our search example.

Example 4.3. Searching the Index and Retrieving Records

```java
import java.io.File;

import org.apache.lucene.analysis.Analyzer;
import org.apache.lucene.analysis.standard.StandardAnalyzer;
import org.apache.lucene.document.Document;
import org.apache.lucene.queryParser.QueryParser;
import org.apache.lucene.search.Hits;
import org.apache.lucene.search.IndexSearcher;
import org.apache.lucene.search.Query;
import org.apache.lucene.store.Directory;
import org.apache.lucene.store.FSDirectory;
import org.marc4j.lucene.RecordUtils;
import org.marc4j.marc.Record;

public class SearchIndexSample {

    public static void main(String args[]) throws Exception {
        if (args.length != 2)
            throw new Exception("Usage: SearchIndexSample " +
                "<index> <term>");

        File indexDir = new File(args[0]);
        String queryString = args[1];

        // create a Lucene index searcher
        Directory dir = FSDirectory.getDirectory(indexDir, false);
        IndexSearcher searcher = new IndexSearcher(dir);

        // search by title
        Analyzer analyzer = new StandardAnalyzer();
        QueryParser parser = new QueryParser("title", analyzer);
        Query q = parser.parse(queryString);
        Hits hits = searcher.search(q);

        for (int i = 0; i < hits.length(); i++) {
            Document doc = hits.doc(i);
            byte[] bytes = doc.getBinaryValue("record");
            Record record = RecordUtils.unmarshal(bytes);
```

```
            System.out.println(record.toString());
        }
    }

}
```

This program writes each record in the search result in tagged display format to standard output:

```
LEADER 00714cam a2200205 a 4500
001 12883376
005 20030616111422.0
008 020805s2002    nyu    j        000 1 eng
020    $a0786808772
020    $a0786816155 (pbk.)
040    $aDLC$cDLC$dDLC
100 1 $aChabon, Michael.
245 10$aSummerland /$cMichael Chabon.
250    $a1st ed.
260    $aNew York :$bMiramax Books/Hyperion Books for Children,$cc2002.
300    $a500 p. ;$c22 cm.
520    $aEthan Feld, the worst baseball player in the history of the game,
   finds himself recruited by a 100-year-old scout to help a band of
   fairies triumph over an ancient enemy.
650    1$aFantasy.
650    1$aBaseball$vFiction.
650    1$aMagic$vFiction.
```

The `QueryParser` requires a default field, but you can also specify the fields in your query to specify other fields than the default field, or to search by multiple fields using boolean operators:

```
// search by creator and title
dc.creator:Chabon AND dc.title:Summerland

// search by creator and title phrase
dc.creator:Chabon AND dc.title:"Kavalier and Clay"

// search by creator and title prase with nested or clause
```

```
dc.creator:Chabon AND (dc.title:"Kavalier and Clay"
  OR dc.title:Summerland)

// search by subject using an or and not clause
dc.subject: (Fantasy OR Magic NOT "Comic books, strips, etc.")
```

Besides the boolean operators, Lucene supports field grouping, wild cards, fuzzy searches and proximity and range searches. Information about the query parser syntax can be found on the Query Parser page. It is available on the website of the Apache Lucene project or in the documentation included in the distribution. I can also recommend *Lucene in Action* by Erik Hatcher and Otis Gospodnetic´.

You can use the Search tab in Luke for experimentation. Make sure to use the same analyzer that was used to create the index. In Example 4.1, "Creating an Index" the StandardAnalyzer was used. The MARC4J Lucene API also provides a command-line utility that enables you create and update a Lucene index for MARC data. See the section called "Indexing MARC with Lucene" in Appendix B, *Command-line Reference* for usage. This command-line utility will be used in Chapter 5, *Putting It All Together* to populate the index for the SRU web application.

Chapter 5. Putting It All Together

Introduction

In this chapter we develop a web application that implements a basic SRU
Search/Retrieve operation. SRU (Search and Retrieve via URL) is a standard search
protocol for Internet search queries. SRU is an XML oriented protocol that allows a user
to search a remote database of records. It uses the Common Query Language (CQL) as a
query language and allows servers to return results marked up in different XML
vocabularies such as Dublin Core, MARCXML or MODS. The design builds on the
experience gained with the Z39.50 information retrieval protocol, but it uses common
Internet standards making it easy to understand and easy to implement.

It is not possible to implement a complete SRU server in a single chapter. The standard is
considered simple, but it is not that simple. The goal of this chapter is to demonstrate
how you can use MARC4J in your applications. The `MarcIndexWriter` will be used to
create the initial index containing indexed MARC records. The MARC4J API will then be
used to serialize results from Lucene to the desired XML output format. Our program
will not have a user interface. The user simply submits a URL based search request to the
server, the server will parse the query to create a Lucene query. Results are returned to
the user in an XML encoded response. Although there are several excellent frameworks
available to create Java web applications, such as the Spring Framework, we will use a
simple application model based on the *Front Controller* pattern as specified in Martin
Fowlers book *Patterns of Enterprise Application Architecture*.

For the previous chapters no specific Java IDE (Integrated Development Environment)
was required, but for this chapter it is strongly recommended to use an IDE such as
Eclipse or IntelliJ IDEA. Since Eclipse is a free IDE, the examples are based on Eclipse,
but if you are an experienced developer, don't hesitate to use the IDE of your choice. To
build and deploy the application, the Eclipse Ant integration is used. Apache Ant is a
build tool written in Java. The application is deployed to the Apache Tomcat servlet
container, but the Search/Retrieve application will also work in other servlet containers.

Setting Up the Environment

If you do not have a copy of Apache Tomcat installed, you can download it at the
Apache Tomcat web site. You can find the installation instructions under the
Documentation section. After installation you can test if Tomcat is running by pointing
the browser to *http://localhost:8080*. If the software was successfully installed you should
see the Apache Tomcat welcome page.

Warning

You must have the CATALINA_HOME environment variable set in order to be able to deploy the Search/Retrieve application. The build.xml file depends on some Apache Tomcat libraries.

Now that we have a target environment, we need to set up a project for development. We need to create the project structure, add the required libraries, configure logging, create a build file, configure some Tomcat tasks and finally create the project in Eclipse. First create the folder structure shown in Figure 5.1, "Project Folder Structure".

Figure 5.1. Project Folder Structure

```
sru
 |
 |--build
 |
 |--src
 |
 |--web
     |
     |--WEB-INF
     |
     |--classes
     |
     |--lib
```

The sru folder is the project root folder containing all the project resources. The src directory is for the Java source code, the build directory is the output directory and the web directory contains the resources that are needed by the servlet container. The web directory has a WEB-INF sub directory that is required by Java web applications. It contains two sub directories: the classes directory contains classes we want to deploy and the lib directory contains the third party libraries.

The Search/Retrieve web application depends on the following third party libraries:

marc4j.jar
    The MARC4J API.

`marc4j-lucene.jar`
>The MARC4J Lucene API.

`cql-java.jar`
>This is a CQL query parser created by Mike Taylor. It is included in the MARC4J Lucene API distribution. It is used to translate CQL query expressions to Lucene query expressions.

`lucene-core-2.0.0.jar`
>The Lucene library that we will use for searching the index created with the MARC4J Lucene API.

`log4j-1.2.8.jar`
>In order to be able to debug the application we will use the Apache Log4j logging services.

Copy these files to the `WEB-INF/lib` directory. To enable logging we need to add a Log4j configuration. If you are familiar with Log4j, you might want to set up your own configuration, otherwise simply copy the lines from Example 5.1, "Basic Log4j Configuration" into a file called `log4j.properties` and save the file in the `classes` directory. It contains a minimalistic configuration to enable Log4j to write log statements to standard output. In Eclipse these statements will be written to the Console View, in Tomcat they will be added to the `stdout.log` file located in the Apache Tomcat `log` directory.

Example 5.1. Basic Log4j Configuration

```
# Set root logger level to DEBUG and its only appender to A1.
log4j.rootLogger=DEBUG, A1

# A1 is set to be a ConsoleAppender.
log4j.appender.A1=org.apache.log4j.ConsoleAppender

# A1 uses PatternLayout.
log4j.appender.A1.layout=org.apache.log4j.PatternLayout
lcg4j.appender.A1.layout.ConversionPattern=%-4r [%t] %-5p %c %x - %m%n

log4j.rootLogger=DEBUG, A1
log4j.appender.A1=org.apache.log4j.ConsoleAppender
log4j.appender.A1.layout=org.apache.log4j.PatternLayout
```

```
# Print the date in ISO 8601 format
log4j.appender.A1.layout.ConversionPattern=%d [%t] %-5p %c - %m%n

# use the A1 appender for our packages
org.marc4j.sru=A1
```

In addition to the WEB-INF directory, the servlet engine requires a *Web Application Deployment Descriptor*. This is an XML file describing the servlets and other components that will make up the Search/Retrieve application. Create a file called web.xml in the WEB-INF directory and add the following:

```xml
<?xml version="1.0" encoding="UTF-8"?>
<web-app xmlns="http://java.sun.com/xml/ns/j2ee"
         xmlns:xsi="http://www.w3.org/2001/XMLSchema-instance"
         xsi:schemaLocation="http://java.sun.com/xml/ns/j2ee http://
         java.sun.com/xml/ns/j2ee/web-app_2_4.xsd" version="2.4">

  <display-name>sru</display-name>

  <!-- servlet configurations -->

</web-app>
```

In order to build and deploy the application, we also need a build file. We use Apache Ant to execute build and deployment tasks. Example 5.2, "The Ant Build File" shows the complete build file for the sru project.

Example 5.2. The Ant Build File

```xml
<?xml version="1.0" encoding="UTF-8"?>
<project name="sru" default="jar" basedir=".">

  <property environment="env" />

  <!-- get the Tomcat home directory -->
  <property name="tomcat.home" value="${env.CATALINA_HOME}" />

  <property name="tomcat.url" value="http://localhost:8080/manager"/>
```

```
<property name="tomcat.username" value="admin"/>
<property name="tomcat.password" value=""/>

<property name="project.name" value="sru"/>
<property name="src.dir" value="src"/>
<property name="web.dir" value="web"/>
<property name="dist.dir" value="dist"/>
<property name="build.dir" value="build"/>
<property name="webapp.name" value="sru"/>

<target name="init">
  <tstamp />
  <record name="build.log" loglevel="verbose" append="no" />
</target>

<path id="classpath">
  <fileset dir="${web.dir}/WEB-INF/lib">
    <include name="*.jar" />
  </fileset>
  <fileset dir="${tomcat.home}/common/lib">
    <include name="servlet*.jar" />
    <include name="mail.jar" />
    <include name="activation.jar" />
  </fileset>
  <pathelement path="${build.dir}" />
  <pathelement path="${web.dir}/WEB-INF/classes" />
</path>

<target name="prepare" depends="init">
  <mkdir dir="${build.dir}" />
</target>

<target name="compile" depends="prepare">
  <javac srcdir="${src.dir}" destdir="${build.dir}">
    <classpath refid="classpath" />
  </javac>
  <copy todir="${build.dir}">
    <fileset dir="${src.dir}">
      <include name="**/*.properties" />
      <include name="**/*.xml" />
    </fileset>
  </copy>
</target>

<target name="jar" depends="compile">
```

```xml
      <jar jarfile="${project.name}.jar">
        <fileset dir="${build.dir}">
          <include name="**/*.class" />
          <include name="**/*.properties" />
          <include name="**/*.xml" />
        </fileset>
      </jar>
  </target>

  <target name="war" depends="compile">
    <mkdir dir="${dist.dir}" />
    <war destfile="${dist.dir}/${webapp.name}.war"
         webxml="${web.dir}/WEB-INF/web.xml">
      <classes dir="${build.dir}" />
      <fileset dir="${web.dir}">
        <include name="**/*.*" />
        <exclude name="**/web.xml" />
      </fileset>
    </war>
  </target>

  <target name="deploy" depends="compile">
    <copy todir="${tomcat.home}/webapps/${webapp.name}"
          preservelastmodified="true">
      <fileset dir="${web.dir}">
        <include name="**/*.*"/>
      </fileset>
    </copy>
    <copy todir="${tomcat.home}/webapps/${webapp.name}/WEB-INF/classes"
          preservelastmodified="true">
      <fileset dir="${build.dir}" />
    </copy>
  </target>

  <target name="clean" depends="init">
    <delete dir="${dist.dir}" />
    <delete dir="${build.dir}" />
  </target>

  <!-- tomcat ant tasks -->
  <taskdef file="tomcatTasks.properties">
    <classpath>
      <pathelement path="${tomcat.home}/server/lib/catalina-ant.jar" />
    </classpath>
  </taskdef>
```

```
    <target name="install" depends="war">
      <deploy url="${tomcat.url}"
              username="${tomcat.username}"
              password="${tomcat.password}"
              path="/${webapp.name}"
              war="file:${dist.dir}/${webapp.name}.war" />
    </target>

    <target name="remove">
      <undeploy url="${tomcat.url}"
                username="${tomcat.username}"
                password="${tomcat.password}"
                path="/${webapp.name}" />
    </target>

    <target name="reload" depends="deploy">
      <reload url="${tomcat.url}"
              username="${tomcat.username}"
              password="${tomcat.password}"
              path="/${webapp.name}" />
    </target>

    <target name="start">
      <start url="${tomcat.url}"
             username="${tomcat.username}"
             password="${tomcat.password}"
             path="/${webapp.name}" />
    </target>

    <target name="stop">
      <stop url="${tomcat.url}"
            username="${tomcat.username}"
            password="${tomcat.password}"
            path="/${webapp.name}" />
    </target>

    <target name="list">
      <list url="${tomcat.url}"
            username="${tomcat.username}"
            password="${tomcat.password}" />
    </target>

</project>
```

Copy these lines into a file called `build.xml` and save the file in the project root folder (this is the `sru` folder).

To run the Apache Tomcat tasks like *deploy*, *undeploy* and *reload*, we need to configure the classes that implement these tasks. To do this, create a file called `tomcatTasks.properties` in the same directory as `build.xml` and add the following lines:

```
deploy=org.apache.catalina.ant.DeployTask
undeploy=org.apache.catalina.ant.UndeployTask
remove=org.apache.catalina.ant.RemoveTask
reload=org.apache.catalina.ant.ReloadTask
start=org.apache.catalina.ant.StartTask
stop=org.apache.catalina.ant.StopTask
list=org.apache.catalina.ant.ListTask
```

The final task, before starting development, is to configure the project in the Eclipse IDE. To do this follow these steps:

Start the New Project wizard

Start Eclipse and select File, New and then Project. Eclipse will show the New Project wizard.

Add the project root folder

Select Java Project and click Next. Eclipse will show the New Java Project wizard. Type `sru` in the Project name input box and then select the Create project from existing source option. Use the Browse button to navigate to the `sru` project root directory and click Next to enter the Java settings.

Add the build path

In the Java settings window, right click on the `src` folder and select the Use as Source Folder option to add the `src` folder to the build path. To add the default output location use the Browse button to select the `build` folder.

Verify if the libraries are added to the CLASSPATH

Click on the Libraries tab to verify if the libraries from the `lib` folder are listed. If this is not the case you can add them using the Add JARs... button.

Add the `classes` folder

Click the Add Class Folder... and navigate to the `WEB-INF` folder. Select the `classes` folder and click OK to add the folder. We need to add the `classes` folder to enable Log4j to find the log appenders.

Add the Apache Tomcat libraries
> We also need some Apache Tomcat libraries. Click Add External JARs and browse on your file system to the `common/lib` folder in the Apache Tomcat home directory. Select the file `servlet-api.jar`. Repeat this last action for `catalina-ant.jar` located in the `server/lib` directory of your Apache Tomcat installation.

Finish the New Project wizard
> Click Finish to save the settings and close the wizard.

Our project is now added to Eclipse. It should look similar to Figure 5.2, "SRU Project in Eclipse":

Figure 5.2. SRU Project in Eclipse

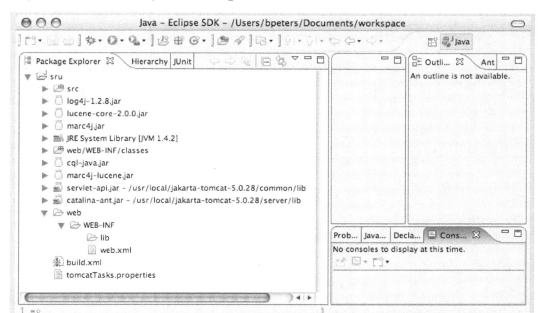

Both the development and deployment environments are now fully configured to start developing the Search/Retrieve application.

Implementing the Controller

The Search/Retrieve application is a web application. It needs to be able to handle HTTP requests from a client such as a browser. It is possible to write a servlet that handles the requests for the Search/Retrieve operation, but since it might be required to implement additional operations in the near future, it is recommended to avoid creating a servlet for each operation. It would introduce all kinds of duplicate behavior across our servlets, such as exception handling when someone requests an operation that is not supported. To avoid this, a single class is created that implements the common behavior to handle all operations, including the Search/Retrieve operation. Example 5.3, "The Controller Class" shows the code for this class.

Example 5.3. The Controller Class

```
package org.marc4j.sru;

import java.io.IOException;
import javax.servlet.ServletConfig;
import javax.servlet.ServletContext;
import javax.servlet.ServletException;
import javax.servlet.http.HttpServlet;
import javax.servlet.http.HttpServletRequest;
import javax.servlet.http.HttpServletResponse;

public class Controller extends HttpServlet {

    private static final String PACKAGE_NAME = "org.marc4j.sru";

    protected ServletContext context;

    public void init(ServletConfig config) throws ServletException {
        context = config.getServletContext();
    }

    public void doGet(HttpServletRequest request,
            HttpServletResponse response)
            throws IOException, ServletException {
        Operation operation = getOperation(request);
        operation.init(context, request, response);
        operation.execute();
    }

    public void doPost(HttpServletRequest request,
            HttpServletResponse response)
            throws IOException, ServletException {
        doGet(request, response);
```

```
    }

    private Operation getOperation(HttpServletRequest request) {
        Operation operation = null;
        try {
            final String actionClassName = PACKAGE_NAME + "."
                    + request.getParameter("operation") + "Operation";

            operation = (Operation) Class.forName(actionClassName)
                    .newInstance();
        } catch (Exception e) {
            operation = new UnsupportedOperation();
        }
        return operation;
    }

    public void destroy() {
        context = null;
    }

}
```

This class extends the `HttpServlet` class. It requires each request to provide a parameter *operation*, representing the SRU operation name, like SearchRetrieve, Explain or Scan. These are operations an SRU server should provide. Based on the *operation* request parameter, the controller tries to instantiate the operation by calling the `getOperation()` method. If there is no match, an `UnsupportedOperation` is instantiated. The controller then initializes the `Operation` instance with the `ServletContext`, the `HttpServletRequest` and `HttpServletResponse` objects. Each operation needs to implement the abstract method `execute()`. This method contains the logic specific to the operation. The `Operation` class also implements a `forward()` method to forward the request to a view. Example 5.4, "The Base Operation Class" shows the abstract `Operation` class.

Example 5.4. The Base Operation Class

```
package org.marc4j.sru;

import java.io.IOException;
```

```
import javax.servlet.RequestDispatcher;
import javax.servlet.ServletContext;
import javax.servlet.ServletException;
import javax.servlet.http.HttpServletRequest;
import javax.servlet.http.HttpServletResponse;

public abstract class Operation {

    protected ServletContext context;

    protected HttpServletRequest request;

    protected HttpServletResponse response;

    public void init(ServletContext context,
            HttpServletRequest request,
            HttpServletResponse response) {
        this.context = context;
        this.request = request;
        this.response = response;
    }

    public abstract public void execute() throws ServletException,
            IOException;

    protected void forward(String target) throws ServletException,
            IOException {
        RequestDispatcher dispatcher =
            context.getRequestDispatcher(target);
        dispatcher.forward(request, response);
    }

}
```

To add these classes to the Search/Retrieve application, we start with adding a package to the `src` folder. Select the `src` folder and click File, New and then Package. Eclipse shows the Java Package window. For the examples in this book I used `org.marc4j.sru`, but you can use a different name. Put the name of your choice in the name field and click Finish. We start with creating the `Operation` class, since the `Controller` class depends on it. To create this class, select the package we just created and then click File, New and then Class. Eclipse shows the Java Class window. Enter `Operation` in the name field and click Finish to create the class. Enter the code listed in

Example 5.4, "The Base Operation Class" and repeat the steps to add a class for the `Controller` class as listed in Example 5.3, "The Controller Class". Make sure to add the `HttpServlet` class in the superclass field when you create the `Controller` class.

Tip

Eclipse can organize the imports for you. When editing a class, either right click on the class in the Package Explorer and go to Source, then Organize Imports or use the command **Ctrl+Shift+O**.

On creation of the `Controller` class, Eclipse reports an error because it cannot locate the `UnsupportedOperation` class. Using an IDE like Eclipse this is easy to solve. Click on the error in the left margin, select the option Create class 'UnsupportedOperation' and click Enter. Eclipse shows the Java Class window. Click Finish to create the class and add the following lines in the body of the `execute()` method:

```
request.setAttribute("code", "4");
request.setAttribute("message", "Unsupported operation");

forward("/diagnostic.jsp");
```

Example 5.5, "The UnsupportedOperation Class." shows the complete code for the `UnsupportedOperation` class.

Example 5.5. The UnsupportedOperation Class.

```
package org.marc4j.sru;

import java.io.IOException;
import javax.servlet.ServletException;

public class UnsupportedOperation extends Operation {

    public void execute() throws ServletException, IOException {
        request.setAttribute("code", "4");
        request.setAttribute("message", "Unsupported operation");

        forward("/diagnostic.jsp");
    }

}
```

When the `Controller` receives a request with an unsupported operation, it will instantiate the `UnsupportedOperation` class and call the `execute()` method. The `UnsupportedOperation` does not have much logic. It simply forwards the request to the `diagnostic.jsp` file. Create this file in the `web` directory and add the JSP code listed in Example 5.6, "Diagnostic Record".

Example 5.6. Diagnostic Record

```
<jsp:root xmlns:jsp="http://java.sun.com/JSP/Page" version="1.2">
<jsp:directive.page contentType="text/xml"/>
<jsp:output omit-xml-declaration="false"/>
<diagnostic xmlns="http://www.loc.gov/zing/srw/diagnostic/">
  <uri>info:srw/diagnostic/1/${requestScope.code}</uri>
  <details>${requestScope.code}</details>
  <message>${requestScope.message}</message>
</diagnostic>
</jsp:root>
```

We now have the `Controller` class, the abstract `Operation` class and a first implementation that is able to handle requests for unsupported operations. When we deploy this web application, it will return an unsupported operation for every request, because it is the only operation currently implemented.

To enable Apache Tomcat to forward requests to the controller, we need to add a servlet mapping to the *Web Application Deployment Descriptor*. Add the following lines to the `web.xml` file located in the `WEB-INF` folder:

```
<servlet>
  <servlet-name>Controller</servlet-name>
  <servlet-class>
    org.marc4j.sru.Controller
  </servlet-class>
  <load-on-startup>1</load-on-startup>
</servlet>

<servlet-mapping>
  <servlet-name>Controller</servlet-name>
  <url-pattern>/search/*</url-pattern>
</servlet-mapping>
```

Example 5.7, "The Deployment Descriptor" shows the complete *Web Application Deployment Descriptor* file.

Example 5.7. The Deployment Descriptor

```xml
<?xml version="1.0" encoding="UTF-8"?>
<web-app xmlns="http://java.sun.com/xml/ns/j2ee"
         xmlns:xsi="http://www.w3.org/2001/XMLSchema-instance"
         xsi:schemaLocation="http://java.sun.com/xml/ns/j2ee http://
         java.sun.com/xml/ns/j2ee/web-app_2_4.xsd" version="2.4">

  <display-name>sru</display-name>

  <servlet>
    <servlet-name>Controller</servlet-name>
    <servlet-class>
      org.marc4j.sru.Controller
    </servlet-class>
    <load-on-startup>1</load-on-startup>
  </servlet>

  <servlet-mapping>
    <servlet-name>Controller</servlet-name>
    <url-pattern>/search/*</url-pattern>
  </servlet-mapping>

</web-app>
```

Since we use a front controller, this is basically all we need to configure in the *Web Application Deployment Descriptor*. If we had used a servlet for each operation, it would have been necessary to configure a servlet every time a new one was added to the application.

You are now ready to deploy the application. In Eclipse select Window, Show View and then Ant. Eclipse opens the Ant View. Click the Add Buildfiles button and select the `build.xml` located in the root folder of the project. Eclipse adds the build file to the Ant View. To test the connection, select the *list* task and click Run the Selected Target. The Eclipse console should list the applications deployed on the Tomcat servlet container:

```
Buildfile: /Users/bpeters/Documents/workspace/sru/build.xml
list:
    [list] OK - Listed applications for virtual host localhost
    [list] /admin:running:0:/usr/local/tomcat/server/webapps/admin
    [list] /balancer:running:0:balancer
    [list] /:running:0:/usr/local/tomcat/webapps/ROOT
    [list] /manager:running:0:/usr/local/tomcat/server/webapps/manager
BUILD SUCCESSFUL
Total time: 1 second
```

Run the *deploy* task to deploy the Search/Retrieve application to Apache Tomcat. When you run the *list* task again, the sru application should appear in the list:

```
Buildfile: /Users/bpeters/Documents/workspace/sru/build.xml
list:
    [list] OK - Listed applications for virtual host localhost
    [list] /admin:running:0:/usr/local/tomcat/server/webapps/admin
    [list] /balancer:running:0:balancer
    [list] /sru:running:0:/usr/local/tomcat/server/webapps/sru
    [list] /:running:0:/usr/local/tomcat/webapps/ROOT
    [list] /manager:running:0:/usr/local/tomcat/server/webapps/manager
BUILD SUCCESSFUL
Total time: 1 second
```

To test the application, open a web browser and enter the following URL:

```
http://localhost:8080/sru/search?operation=SearchRetrieve
```

The browser should display the following diagnostic message:

```
<?xml version="1.0" encoding="UTF-8"?>
<diagnostic xmlns="http://www.loc.gov/zing/srw/diagnostic/">
  <uri>info:srw/diagnostic/1/4</uri>
  <details>4</details>
  <message>Unsupported operation.</message>
</diagnostic>
```

Building the Index

Before we continue development, we first need to populate an Apache Lucene index. You can use the `MarcIndexDriver` to do that. This class is a command-line program that can add records to either a new Lucene index or an existing one. To run the driver, the following libraries are required on the CLASSPATH environment variable:

```
marc4j.jar
lucene-core-2.0.0.jar
marc4j-lucene.jar
commons-logging-1.1.jar
```

You need some MARC records, but I assume that will be no problem, since that's what this book is all about. Creating the index is very simple. Create a directory called `index` as a subdirectory of `sru`, the project root directory. The following command creates the index in directory `/Users/bpeters/Documents/workspace/sru/index` and adds the given MARC records:

```
java -jar marc4j-lucene.jar
  -index /Users/bpeters/Documents/workspace/sru/index
  -create input.mrc
```

Running this command from the command-line will output something similar to this:

```
Index has 0 documents
Added 2 documents in 410 milliseconds
```

You can also specify the CLASSPATH and main class explicitly using a command of the form:

```
java -cp marc4j.jar;lucene-core-2.0.0.jar;marc4j-lucene.jar;
  commons-logging-1.1.jar org.marc4j.lucene.util.MarcIndexDriver
  -index /Users/bpeters/Documents/workspace/sru/index -create input.mrc
```

Warning

If you add multiple files to the index use the **-create** option only for the first file, otherwise `MarcIndexDriver` will overwrite the existing index every time you add a new file.

Implementing the SRU Operation

Now that we have the controller framework and a Lucene index that contains some records, we can start developing the Search/Retrieve operation. We start with developing a simple gateway to wrap the specific Lucene code. Example 5.8, "The SearchGateway Class" implements the logic needed for the Search/Retrieve operation.

Example 5.8. The SearchGateway Class

```
package org.marc4j.sru;

import java.io.IOException;

import org.apache.log4j.Logger;
import org.apache.lucene.analysis.Analyzer;
import org.apache.lucene.analysis.standard.StandardAnalyzer;
import org.apache.lucene.queryParser.QueryParser;
import org.apache.lucene.search.Hits;
import org.apache.lucene.search.IndexSearcher;
import org.apache.lucene.search.Query;
import org.apache.lucene.store.Directory;
import org.apache.lucene.store.FSDirectory;
import org.marc4j.lucene.util.QueryHelper;

public class SearchGateway {

    static Logger log = Logger.getLogger(SearchGateway.class);

    // location of the index
    public static final String INDEX_DIR =
      "/Users/bpeters/Documents/workspace/sru/index";

    public Hits query(String cql) throws IOException {
        log.debug("entering query() method");
```

```
Directory dir = FSDirectory.getDirectory(INDEX_DIR, false);
IndexSearcher searcher = new IndexSearcher(dir);

Analyzer analyzer = new StandardAnalyzer();
QueryParser parser = new QueryParser("dc:title", analyzer);
Query q = null;
try {
    // create Lucene expression from CQL expression
    String queryString = QueryHelper.toLucene(cql);
    log.debug("Lucene query expression: " + queryString);

    q = parser.parse(queryString);
} catch (Exception e) {
    log.error(e.getMessage(), e);
}

Hits hits = searcher.search(q);
log.debug("Hits returned for " + cql + ": " + hits.length());

return hits;
}

}
```

Most of the code in Example 5.8, "The SearchGateway Class" is similar to Example 4.2, "Searching the Index" in Chapter 4, *Indexing with Lucene*. The IndexSearcher instance uses the FSDirectory object to open the directory containing the index. The StandardAnalyzer is used to analyze the search query string to ensure that the query is in the same form as the index. A part that needs some explanation is the following line of code:

```
String queryString = QueryHelper.toLucene(cql);
```

The QueryHelper class is part of the MARC4J Lucene library. It enables you to translate a CQL query expression to a Lucene query expression, but it only supports a limited set of features required by CQL. In the current release the QueryHelper class supports the query expressions listed in Table 5.1, "Query Examples".

Table 5.1. Query Examples

CQL Query Expression	Description
`Summerland`	Matches records that contain `Summerland` in the default field.
`dc.title = Summerland`	Matches records that contain the term `Summerland` in the `dc.title` field.
`dc.title = "Kavalier and Clay"`	Matches records that contain the phrase `"Kavalier and Clay"` in the `dc.title` field.
`dc.author = Chabon and "Kavalier and Clay"`	Matches records that contain the term `Chabon` in the `dc.creator` field and the phrase `"Kavalier and Clay"` in the default field.
`Summerland or "Kavalier and Clay"`	Matches records that contain the term `Summerland` or the phrase `"Kavalier and Clay"` in the default field.
`dc.subject = (Fantasy or Magic) not "Comic books, strips, etc."`	Matches records that contain the term `Fantasy` or `Magic`, but not the phrase `"Comic books, strips, etc."` in the `dc.subject` field.

You can use the wildcards * (match zero or more characters) and ? (match a single character).

The `Query` object is created using the Lucene query string returned by the `toLucene()` method. The `IncexSearcher` instance uses the `Query` instance and returns a `Hits` object that contains documents that meet the criteria.

Note

In a real world application it is not recommended to create a new instance of `IndexSearcher` every time the `query()` method is executed, but for now this will work. It is also recommended to put the location of the index in a property file located cn the CLASSPATH environment to avoid having to update the class when the location of the index changes.

To test the gateway, we add a JUnit test class to the project. JUnit is a Java library to run automated tests. It is an essential tool for Java developers and most IDE's enable you to run tests from within the editor. It is not the purpose of this book to provide a tutorial on how to use JUnit. There are quite a few books and online tutorials available that cover this subject. Before we can start writing test classes, we need to add the `junit.jar` to the CLASSPATH. In Eclipse select Project, then Properties from the menu. Then go to the Libraries tab, click Add External JARs... and navigate to the directory where you installed Eclipse. Go to the sub directory `plugins` and then to a sub directory that is called something like `org.junit_3.8.1`. Open this directory, select `junit.jar` and click open to add the library to the CLASSPATH environment variable. Example 5.9, "JUnit Test for Gateway" shows the code for the JUnit test to test the `query()` method in the `SearchGateway` class.

Example 5.9. JUnit Test for Gateway

```
package org.marc4j.sru.test;

import junit.framework.TestCase;
import org.apache.lucene.search.Hits;
import org.marc4j.sru.SearchGateway;

public class SearchGatewayTest extends TestCase {

    public void testSimpleQuery() throws Exception {
        SearchGateway gateway = new SearchGateway();
        Hits hits = gateway.query("Summerland");
        assertEquals(1, hits.length());
    }

}
```

The JUnit `TestCase` class provides test methods like `assertEquals()` to test if a particular condition is true. If this is not the case, the test fails. You can run the test from within your Eclipse environment. Right click on the test class and select Run As... and then JUnit Test. JUnit will run every method in the class that starts with `test`. In this case there is only one test method called `testSimpleQuery()`. It assumes there is an indexed record with title *Summerland*.

We are now ready to implement the Search/Retrieve operation. It will use the `SearchGateway` class to execute queries. Select the package `org.marc4j.sru` and then select File, New, Class. Add `SearchRetrieveOperation` in the name field and add `Operation` as a superclass. Click finish to create the class. Example 5.10, "The SearchRetrieveOperation Class" shows the code created by Eclipse.

Example 5.10. The SearchRetrieveOperation Class

```
package org.marc4j.sru;

import java.io.IOException;
import javax.servlet.ServletException;

public class SearchRetrieveOperation extends Operation {

    public void execute() throws ServletException, IOException {
        // TODO Auto-generated method stub
    }

}
```

We will start with a first implementation that simply returns the number of records retrieved by the query. Example 5.11, "Method Implementation" shows the code for this implementation.

Example 5.11. Method Implementation

```
package org.marc4j.sru;

import java.io.IOException;
import java.io.PrintWriter;

import javax.servlet.ServletException;

import org.apache.lucene.search.Hits;

public class SearchRetrieveOperation extends Operation {

    public void execute() throws ServletException, IOException {

        String queryString = request.getParameter("query");

        SearchGateway gateway = new SearchGateway();
        Hits hits = gateway.query(queryString);
```

```
        response.setContentType("text/xml;charset=utf-8");

        PrintWriter writer = response.getWriter();

        writer.println("<?xml version=\"1.0\" encoding=\"UTF-8\"?>");
        writer.println("<searchRetrieveResponse "
            + "xmlns=\"http://www.loc.gov/zing/srw/\">\n"
            + "  <version>1.1</version>\n  <numberOfRecords>"
            + hits.length() + "</numberOfRecords>\n"
            + "</searchRetrieveResponse>");
        writer.flush();
    }

}
```

The *query* parameter is retrieved from the request and used to obtain a `Hits` object using the `SearchGateway`. The browser needs to know that it will receive an XML encoded response. This is done using the `setContentType` method. The response is returned via the `PrintWriter` object that is obtained from the `HttpServletResponse`. To test the `SearchRetrieveOperation`, deploy and reload the application using the Ant tasks, open a web browser and enter the following URL:

```
http://localhost:8080/sru/search?operation=SearchRetrieve
    &query=Summerland
```

If you enter a title word that matches one or more titles in your Lucene index, the operation should return a response similar to this:

```
<?xml version="1.0" encoding="UTF-8"?>
<searchRetrieveResponse xmlns="http://www.loc.gov/zing/srw/">
  <version>1.1</version>
  <numberOfRecords>1</numberOfRecords>
</searchRetrieveResponse>
```

The next part is adding the actual records from the search result to the response. According to the SRU standard, each record should be embedded in a *record* element like this:

```
<record>
  <recordPacking>XML</recordPacking>
  <recordSchema>info:srw/schema/1/dc-v1.1</recordSchema>
  <recordData>
    <!-- the record data -->
  </recordData>
  <recordNumber>1</recordNumber>
</record>
```

The *record* element provides information about the data format and structure of the embedded record. In this case the record is encoded in XML according to the Dublin Core schema.

There are a few things to consider for the Search/Retrieve response. We could simply continue with the current approach and use the `println()` method of our response writer to write the whole XML response as a `String`, but then we would end up with unreadable code that is difficult to maintain. A better approach is using one of the XML API's, for example to create a DOM `Document` instance and serialize the document to the response writer. As an alternative, we can also develop an XSLT stylesheet to create the response and use `MarcXmlWriter` to write the result to the response writer. Another alternative is to implement a new `MarcWriter` implementation that uses the low-level SAX interface to produce the XML output using SAX events. This approach was used for Example 3.6, "Dublin Core Writer". For a high traffic SRU server this might be the best solution, but for now let's use an XSLT stylesheet to create the response.

We start with creating a basic stylesheet that transforms MARCXML to a limited Dublin Core document with only a *creator* and *title* element. Copy the contents of listing Example 5.12, "The Dublin Core Stylesheet" in a file called `marcxml2dc.xsl` and add the file to the `org.marc4j.sru` package in a sub directory called `resources`.

Example 5.12. The Dublin Core Stylesheet

```
<?xml version="1.0" encoding="utf-8"?>
<xsl:stylesheet version="1.0"
              xmlns="http://www.loc.gov/zing/srw"
              xmlns:marc="http://www.loc.gov/MARC21/slim"
              xmlns:srw_dc="info:srw/schema/1/dc-schema"
              xmlns:dc="http://purl.org/dc/elements/1.1/"
              xmlns:xsl="http://www.w3.org/1999/XSL/Transform"
              exclude-result-prefixes="marc">
```

```xsl
<xsl:output method="xml" indent="yes" encoding="UTF-8"/>

<xsl:template match="/">
  <searchRetrieveResponse
      xmlns="http://www.loc.gov/zing/srw/"
      xmlns:dc="http://purl.org/dc/elements/1.1/">
    <version>1.1</version>
    <numberOfRecords>
      <xsl:value-of select="count(//marc:record)"/>
    </numberOfRecords>
    <xsl:apply-templates/>
  </searchRetrieveResponse>
</xsl:template>

<xsl:template match="marc:record">
  <record>
    <recordPacking>XML</recordPacking>
    <recordSchema>info:srw/schema/1/dc-v1.1</recordSchema>
    <recordData>
      <srw_dc:dc>
        <xsl:call-template name="creator"/>
        <xsl:call-template name="title"/>
      </srw_dc:dc>
    </recordData>
    <recordNumber><xsl:number/></recordNumber>
  </record>
</xsl:template>

<xsl:template name="creator">
  <dc:creator>
    <xsl:for-each select="marc:datafield[@tag=100]">
      <xsl:call-template name="writeSubfields"/>
    </xsl:for-each>
  </dc:creator>
</xsl:template>

<xsl:template name="title">
  <dc:title>
    <xsl:for-each select="marc:datafield[@tag=245]">
      <xsl:call-template name="writeSubfields">
        <xsl:with-param name="codes">abfghk</xsl:with-param>
      </xsl:call-template>
    </xsl:for-each>
  </dc:title>
```

```
    </xsl:template>

    <xsl:template name="writeSubfields">
      <xsl:param name="codes">abcdefghijklmnopqrstuvwxyz</xsl:param>
        <xsl:for-each select="marc:subfield">
          <xsl:if test="contains($codes, @code)">
            <xsl:if test="position() > 1">
              <xsl:text> </xsl:text>
            </xsl:if>
            <xsl:value-of select="text()"/>
          </xsl:if>
        </xsl:for-each>
    </xsl:template>

</xsl:stylesheet>
```

To update the `execute()` method, first remove all the code under the line where the response writer gets retrieved using the `getWriter()` method call. We start with creating a `Source` object containing the stylesheet:

```
String stylesheetPath = "resources/marcxml2dc.xsl";
InputStream in = getClass().getResourceAsStream(stylesheetPath);
Source source = new StreamSource(in);
```

The `getResourceAsStream()` method is used to locate the file containing the stylesheet relative to the location of the `SearchRetrieveOperation` class. To avoid having to re-parse the stylesheet for every request, it is recommended to create a `Templates` object and cache it in the `ServletContext`, but for now this will work. Next create a `Result` object containing the response writer. The stylesheet output will be written to this writer.

```
Result result = new StreamResult(writer);
```

The `Result` and `Source` instances are used to create an instance of `MarcXmlWriter`:

```
MarcWriter marcWriter = new MarcXmlWriter(result, source);
```

You can then read records from the search result by iterating over the `Hits` to retrieve the ISO 2709 byte stream from the `Document`:

```
for (int i = 0; i < hits.length(); i++) {
    Document doc = hits.doc(i);

    // write each record
}
```

The MARC4J Lucene API provides a class called `RecordUtils` that is able to unmarshal the byte stream to a `Record` object:

```
byte[] bytes = doc.getBinaryValue("record");
Record record = RecordUtils.unmarshal(bytes);
```

Each record is written to the `MarcWriter` implementation that writes output to the servlet response:

```
marcWriter.write(record);
```

Finally you need to close the `MarcWriter` instance and flush the response writer. Example 5.13, "The Updated Method" shows the complete code for the updated `execute()` method.

Example 5.13. The Updated Method

```
public void execute() throws ServletException, IOException {

    String queryString = request.getParameter("query");

    SearchGateway gateway = new SearchGateway();
    Hits hits = gateway.query(queryString);

    response.setContentType("text/xml;charset=utf-8");
```

```java
        PrintWriter writer = response.getWriter();

        String stylesheetPath = "resources/marcxml2dc.xsl";
        InputStream in = getClass().getResourceAsStream(stylesheetPath);
        Source source = new StreamSource(in);

        Result result = new StreamResult(writer);

        MarcWriter marcWriter = new MarcXmlWriter(result, source);
        for (int i = 0; i < hits.length(); i++) {
            Document doc = hits.doc(i);
            byte[] bytes = doc.getBinaryValue("record");
            Record record = RecordUtils.unmarshal(bytes);
            marcWriter.write(record);
        }
        marcWriter.close();

        writer.flush();
}
```

Deploy and reload the application using the Ant tasks, open a web browser and enter the following URL:

```
http://localhost:8080/sru/search?operation=SearchRetrieve
  &query=Summerland
```

If you enter a title word that matches one or more titles in your Lucene index, the operation should return a response similar to this:

```xml
<?xml version="1.0" encoding="UTF-8"?>
<searchRetrieveResponse xmlns="http://www.loc.gov/zing/srw/"
                        xmlns:srw_dc="info:srw/schema/1/dc-schema"
                        xmlns:dc="http://purl.org/dc/elements/1.1/">
  <version>1.1</version>
  <numberOfRecords>1</numberOfRecords>
  <record xmlns="http://www.loc.gov/zing/srw">
    <recordPacking>XML</recordPacking>
    <recordSchema>info:srw/schema/1/dc-v1.1</recordSchema>
    <recordData>
```

```
      <srw_dc:dc>
        <dc:creator>Chabon, Michael.</dc:creator>
        <dc:title>Summerland /</dc:title>
      </srw_dc:dc>
    </recordData>
    <recordNumber>1</recordNumber>
  </record>
</searchRetrieveResponse>
```

Most browsers automatically encode characters that need to be escaped in a URL, so you should also be able to execute more complex queries like for example:

```
http://localhost:8080/sru/search?operation=SearchRetrieve&query=
  dc.creator="Chabon, Michael" and "Kavalier and Clay"
```

You can now add templates to the XSLT stylesheet to include other Dublin Core fields in the response. To do this, first add templates for each field you want to add, like for example to add the publisher and publication date:

```
<xsl:template name="publisher">
  <xsl:for-each select="marc:datafield[@tag=260]">
    <dc:publisher>
      <xsl:call-template name="writeSubfields">
        <xsl:with-param name="codes">ab</xsl:with-param>
      </xsl:call-template>
    </dc:publisher>
  </xsl:for-each>
</xsl:template>

<xsl:template name="date">
  <xsl:for-each select="marc:datafield[@tag=260]">
    <dc:date>
      <xsl:value-of select="marc:subfield[@code='c']"/>
    </dc:date>
  </xsl:for-each>
</xsl:template>
```

Then add a call to the new templates in the template that matches the *record* element:

```
<xsl:call-template name="publisher"/>
<xsl:call-template name="date"/>
```

The reason we explicitly call each template, is that otherwise we will end up with the remaining data from the source tree in the response. You can test this by replacing the *call-template* elements with an empty *apply-templates* element:

```
<xsl:template match="marc:record">
  <record>
    <recordPacking>XML</recordPacking>
    <recordSchema>info:srw/schema/1/dc-v1.1</recordSchema>
    <recordData>
      <srw_dc:dc>
        <xs:apply-templates/>
      </srw_dc:dc>
    </recordData>
    <recordNumber><xsl:number/></recordNumber>
  </record>
</xsl:template>
```

Adding the Explain Operation

The Explain operation records the facilities that are available on the SRU server. It can be used for configuration purposes by the client and contains such information as the host, port and path and the record schema used by the Search/Retrieve operation. The explain response should be returned when the client simply sends a request to the SRU database, in our case:

```
http://localhost:8080/sru
```

To do this, create another JSP template containing the explain response and add this template to the web.xml file as a welcome file. Add the contents of Example 5.14, "JSP Template for the Explain Response" to a file called explain.jsp and save the file in the web directory.

Example 5.14. JSP Template for the Explain Response

```
<jsp:root xmlns:jsp="http://java.sun.com/JSP/Page"
          version="1.2">
  <jsp:output omit-xml-declaration="false"/>
  <jsp:directive.page contentType="text/xml"/>
  <explainResponse xmlns="http://www.loc.gov/zing/srw/"
                    xmlns:zr="http://explain.z3950.org/dtd/2.0/">
    <version>1.1</version>
    <record>
      <recordPacking>XML</recordPacking>
      <recordSchema>http://explain.z3950.org/dtd/2.0/ </recordSchema>
      <recordData>
        <zr:explain>
          <zr:serverInfo>
            <zr:host>localhost</zr:host>
            <zr:port>8080</zr:port>
            <zr:database>sru/search</zr:database>
          </zr:serverInfo>
          <zr:databaseInfo>
            <zr:title>An example SRU service</zr:title>
            <zr:description lang='en' primary='true'>
              This is an example SRU service.
            </zr:description>
          </zr:databaseInfo>
          <zr:schemaInfo>
            <zr:schema identifier='info:srw/schema/1/dc-v1.1'
                       sort='false' name='dc'>
              <zr:title>Dublin Core</zr:title>
            </zr:schema>
          </zr:schemaInfo>
          <zr:configInfo>
            <zr:default type='numberOfRecords'>100</zr:default>
          </zr:configInfo>
        </zr:explain>
      </recordData>
    </record>
  </explainResponse>
</jsp:root>
```

To add the explain response as a welcome file, open the `web.xml` file and add the following lines under the Servlet mappings:

```
<welcome-file-list>
  <welcome-file>explain.jsp</welcome-file>
</welcome-file-list>
```

Deploy and reload the application using the Ant tasks, open a web browser and enter the following URL:

```
http://localhost:8080/sru
```

You should see the contents of the explain response document.

In addition to the application URL, the explain operation should also be the response of an operation URL. For our application this means that the following URL should return the explain response:

```
http://localhost:8080/sru/search?version=1.1&operation=Explain
```

Thanks to our controller this is not difficult. Adding an operation class called `ExplainOperation` with a forward to the `explain.jsp` should be enough. Example 5.15, "The ExplainOperation Class" shows the complete code.

Example 5.15. The ExplainOperation Class

```
package org.marc4j.sru;

import java.io.IOException;

import javax.servlet.ServletException;

public class ExplainOperation extends Operation {

    public void execute() throws ServletException, IOException {
        forward("/explain.jsp");
```

```
        }

    }
```

Deploy and reload the application using the Ant tasks, open a web browser and enter the following URL:

```
http://localhost:8080/sru/search?version=1.1&operation=Explain
```

Again you should see the contents of the explain response document.

We now have a basic SRU implementation that provides support for the Search/Retrieve operation and is able to report the facilities to the client. The implementation is fully functional, but it does not support all the request parameters specified by the Search/Retrieve operation and CQL support is limited to the use of boolean operators and wild cards. In a production environment an SRU server should also report more detailed diagnostics and the standard specifies a third operation, the Scan operation, to enable clients to browse the index for search terms.

Is Java still suitable for web application development? Recently there has been a lot of discussion about Java as a platform for web applications. The Java 2 Enterprise Edition (J2EE), Sun's platform for web applications, has evolved into a complex platform, especially for applications that do not require the enterprise scalability and security that J2EE provides. Open source projects such as Hibernate and the Spring Framework show that you do not need traditional J2EE application models to solve complex real-world problems. The solution presented here is not ready for deployment in a production environment, but it required only 216 lines of code and a few simple Java Server Pages to implement a working SRU server.

Appendix A. MARC4J API Summary

This appendix provides a quick reference to the MARC4J API. It provides a brief overview for the core interfaces and classes.

The org.marc4j Package

The `org.marc4j` package holds the interfaces and classes for reading and writing MARC and MARCXML data.

MarcReader

Implement this interface to provide an iterator over a collection of `Record` objects.

`hasNext()`
: Returns true if the iteration has more records, false otherwise.

`next()`
: Returns the next record in the iteration.

MARC4J provides two `MarcReader` implementations:

`MarcStreamReader`
: An iterator over a collection of MARC records in ISO 2709 format.

`MarcXmlReader`
: An iterator over a collection of MARC records in MARCXML format.

MarcWriter

Implement this interface to provide a writer for `Record` objects.

`close()`
: Closes the writer.

`getConverter()`
: Returns the character converter.

```
setConverter(CharConverter converter)
```
Sets the character converter.

```
write(Record record)
```
Writes a single Record to the output stream.

MARC4J provides two `MarcWriter` implementations:

```
MarcStreamWriter
```
Class for writing MARC record objects in ISO 2709 format.

```
MarcXmlWriter
```
Class for writing MARC record objects in MARCXML format.

The org.marc4j.marc Package

The `org.marc4j.marc` package holds the interfaces that incorporate the behaviour and data of a MARC record and contains the default implementation of this domain model.

Record

Represents a MARC record.

```
addVariableField(VariableField field)
```
Adds a `VariableField` object.

```
find(String pattern)
```
Returns a `List` of `VariableField` objects that have a data element that matches the given regular expression.

```
find(String[] tag, String pattern)
```
Returns a `List` of `VariableField` objects with the given tags that have a data element that matches the given regular expression.

```
find(String tag, String pattern)
```
Returns a `List` of `VariableField` objects with the given tag that have a data element that matches the given regular expression.

```
getControlFields()
```
Returns a `List` of control fields

`getControlNumber()`
Returns the control number or null if no control number is available.

`getControlNumberField()`
Returns the control number field or null if no control number field is available.

`getDataFields()`
Returns a list of data fields

`getLeader()`
Returns the Leader.

`getType()`
Returns the type of record.

`getVariableField(String tag)`
Returns the first instance of `VariableField` with the given tag.

`getVariableFields()`
Returns a `List` of variable fields

`getVariableFields(String tag)`
Returns a `List` of variable fields with the given tag.

`getVariableFields(String[] tag)`
Returns a `List` of `VariablField` objects for the given tags.

`removeVariableField(VariableField field)`
Removes a variable field from the collection. Use this method to remove fields obtained from a `getVariableFields()` method.

`setLeader(Leader leader)`
Sets the `Leader` object.

`setType(String type)`
Sets the type of record.

Leader

Represents a record label in a MARC record.

`getBaseAddressOfData()`
Returns the base address of data (positions 12-16).

`getCharCodingScheme()`
　　Returns the character coding scheme (position 09).

`getEntryMap()`
　　Returns the entry map (positions 20-23).

`getImplDefined1()`
　　Returns implementation defined values (positions 07-08).

`getImplDefined2()`
　　Returns implementation defined values (positions 17-19).

`getIndicatorCount()`
　　Returns the indicator count (positions 10).

`getRecordLength()`
　　Returns the logical record length (positions 00-04).

`getRecordStatus()`
　　Returns the record status (positions 05).

`getSubfieldCodeLength()`
　　Returns the subfield code length (position 11).

`getTypeOfRecord()`
　　Returns the record type (position 06).

`marshal()`
　　Creates a `String` object from this `Leader` object.

`setBaseAddressOfData(int baseAddressOfData)`
　　Sets the base address of data (positions 12-16).

`setCharCodingScheme(char charCodingScheme)`
　　Sets the character encoding scheme (position 09).

`setEntryMap(char[] entryMap)`
　　Sets the entry map (positions 20-23).

`setImplDefined1(char[] implDefined1)`
　　Sets implementation defined values (position 07-08).

`setImplDefined2(char[] implDefined2)`
　　Sets implementation defined values (positions 17-19).

```
setIndicatorCount(int indicatorCount)
```
Sets the indicator count (position 10).

```
setRecordLength(int recordLength)
```
Sets the logical record length (positions 00-04).

```
setRecordStatus(char recordStatus)
```
Sets the record status (position 05).

```
setSubfieldCodeLength(int subfieldCodeLength)
```
Sets the subfield code length (position 11).

```
setTypeOfRecord(char typeOfRecord)
```
Sets the type of record (position 06).

```
unmarshal(String ldr)
```
Creates a `Leader` object from a `String` object.

VariableField

Represents a variable field in a MARC record.

```
find(String pattern)
```
Returns `true` if the given regular expression matches a subsequence of a data element within the variable field.

```
getTag()
```
Returns the tag name.

```
setTag(String tag)
```
Sets the tag name.

ControlField

Represents a control field in a MARC record.

```
getData()
```
Returns the data element as a `String` object.

```
setData(String data)
```
Sets the data element.

DataField

Represents a data field in a MARC record.

`addSubfield(int index, Subfield subfield)`
Inserts a Subfield at the specified position.

`addSubfield(Subfield subfield)`
Adds a Subfield.

`getIndicator1()`
Returns the first indicator.

`getIndicator2()`
Returns the second indicator.

`getSubfield(char code)`
Returns the first `Subfield` object with the given code.

`getSubfields()`
Returns the list of `Subfield` objects.

`getSubfields(char code)`
Returns the list of Subfield objects for the given subfield code.

`removeSubfield(Subfield subfield)`
Removes a Subfield.

`setIndicator1(char ind1)`
Sets the first indicator.

`setIndicator2(char ind2)`
Sets the second indicator.

Subfield

Represents a subfield in a MARC record.

`find(String pattern)`
Returns true if the given regular expression matches a subsequence of the data element.

```
getCode()
```
Returns the data element identifier.

```
getData()
```
Returns the data element.

```
setCode(char code)
```
Sets the data element identifier.

```
setData(String data)
```
Sets the data element.

MarcFactory

Factory for creating MARC record objects.

```
newControlField()
```
Returns a new control field instance.

```
newControlField(String tag)
```
Creates a new control field with the given tag and returns the instance.

```
newControlField(String tag, String data)
```
Creates a new control field with the given tag and data and returns the instance.

```
newDataField()
```
Returns a new data field instance.

```
newDataField(String tag, char ind1, char ind2)
```
Creates a new data field with the given tag and indicators and returns the instance.

```
newInstance()
```
Creates a new factory instance.

```
newLeader()
```
Returns a new leader instance.

```
newLeader(String ldr)
```
Creates a new leader with the given String object.

```
newRecord()
```
Returns a new record instance.

```
newRecord(Leader leader)
```
Returns a new record instance.

```
newRecord(String leader)
```
Returns a new record instance.

```
newSubfield()
```
Returns a new subfield instance.

```
newSubfield(char code)
```
Creates a new subfield with the given identifier.

```
newSubfield(char code, String data)
```
Creates a new subfield with the given identifier and data.

The org.marc4j.converter Package

This package contains the interface for the character converter

CharConverter

Implement this class to create a character converter.

```
convert(String dataElement)
```
Converts the dataElement and returns the result as a String object.

The package `org.marc4j.converter.impl` provides default implementations for three character encodings through the following classes:

```
AnselToUnicode
```
A utility to convert MARC-8 data to non-precomposed UCS/Unicode.

```
UnicodeToAnsel
```
A utility to convert UCS/Unicode data to MARC-8.

```
Iso5426ToUnicode
```
A utility to convert UNIMARC data to UCS/Unicode.

```
UnicodeToIso5426
```
A utility to convert UCS/Unicode data to UNIMARC (ISO 5426 charset).

`Iso6937ToUnicode`
> A utility to convert ISO 6937 data to UCS/Unicode.

`UnicodeToIso6937`
> A utility to convert UCS/Unicode data to ISO 6937.

The org.marc4j.util Package

This package contains the command-line utilities. See Appendix B, *Command-line Reference* for usage.

`MarcXmlDriver`
> Provides a basic driver to convert MARC records to MARCXML.

`XmlMarcDriver`
> Provides a driver to convert MARCXML records to MARC format.

The org.marc4j.lucene Package

The `org.marc4j.lucene` package provides a `MarcWriter` implementation to index MARC data using the Lucene search engine.

MarcIndexWriter

Class for writing Record objects to a Lucene index based on a Lucene document configuration for MARC records. The constructor takes an instance of `org.apache.lucene.index.IndexWriter` and an optional MARC4J Indexing Schema file as arguments.

`close()`
> Closes the index writer.

`getConverter()`
> Returns the character converter.

`setConverter(CharConverter converter)`
> Sets the character converter.

`setUnicodeNormalization(boolean normalize)`
> If set to true this writer will perform Unicode normalization on data elements using normalization form C (NFC).

`write(Record record)`
> Creates a Lucene document and adds it to the index.

The org.marc4j.lucene.util Package

The `org.marc4j.lucene.util` contains some helper classes and the command-utility to create an index based on MARC records.

`MarcIndexDriver`
> Provides a basic driver to create a Lucene index for MARC records. See Appendix B, *Command-line Reference* for usage.

RecordUtils

Helper class for serializing and deserializing records.

`marshal(Record record)`
> Serializes the given Record object to a byte stream in ISO 2709 format.

`marshal(Record record, CharConverter converter, String encoding)`
> Serializes the given Record object to a byte stream in ISO 2709 format.

`marshal(Record record, String encoding)`
> Serializes the given Record object to a byte stream in ISO 2709 format.

`toXML(Record record, OutputStream out)`
> Serializes a record to MARCXML.

`toXML(Record record, String stylesheetUrl, OutputStream out)`
> Serializes a record to MARCXML and then applies the given stylesheet.

`unmarshal(byte[] bytes)`
> Builds a Record object from the given byte stream in ISO 2709 format.

`unmarshal(byte[] bytes, String encoding)`
> Builds a Record object from the given byte stream in ISO 2709 format.

QueryHelper

Helper class to convert a CQL query to a Lucene query. This class requires the `cql-java.jar` package.

`toLucene(String cql)`
> Converts the given CQL query string to a Lucene query string.

`toLuceneQuery(String cql)`
> Converts the given CQL query string to a Lucene Query object.

Appendix B. Command-line Reference

MARC4J provides a command line interface through two Java classes. To use them you need a Java Virtual Machine and the MARC4J distribution. Make sure to add both `marc4j.jar` and `normalizer.jar` to the CLASSPATH environment variable. The `MarcXmlDriver` class can be used to convert a file containing MARC records to MARCXML or to a different format, like MODS or Dublin Core, by processing the result through an XSLT. The `XmlMarcDriver` class can be used to convert a file containing MARCXML data back to MARC in ISO 2709 format. It is also possible to process the input source through XSLT to create MARCXML from a different source format, like MODS or Dublin Core. The MARC4J Lucene package provides a command line utility to create a Lucene index holding MARC data.

MARC to XML

The `MarcXmlDriver` requires an input file containing one or more MARC records in ISO 2709 format. In addition the class takes zero or more of the following options:

-usage
> Show the usage text.

-out *output-file*
> Specify the name of the output file. If this argument is not present output is written to the console.

-convert *encoding*
> Convert the data elements to UTF-8 using the given encoding. MARC4J supports the following encodings:
>
> * *MARC8* (MARC-8 ANSEL used by MARC 21)
>
> * *ISO5426* (ISO 5426 used by UNIMARC records)
>
> * *ISO6937* (ISO 6937 used by UNIMARC records)

-encoding
> Decode the input stream using the given encoding name. Use Java encoding names such as UTF8 and ISO8859_1. The default character encoding is Latin 1 (ISO8859_1).

-normalize
> Perform Unicode normalization. With Unicode normalization text is transformed into the canonical composed form. For example "a´bc" is normalized to "ábc".

-xsl *stylesheet*

Process the result through an XSLT stylesheet located at the given URL. The stylesheet should consume well-formed MARCXML data.

The examples below assume that you use Sun's Java Virtual Machine. The following command simply converts the given file with MARC records to MARCXML and writes output to the "standard" output stream:

```
java org.marc4j.util.MarcXmlDriver input.mrc
```

To write the result to a file add a file name and optional path:

```
java org.marc4j.util.MarcXmlDriver -out output.xml input.mrc
```

To convert MARC 21 records encoded in MARC-8 ANSEL to UTF-8 add the **-convert** argument with the *MARC8* encoding value:

```
java org.marc4j.util.MarcXmlDriver -convert MARC8
  -out output.xml input.mrc
```

To perform Unicode normalization:

```
java org.marc4j.util.MarcXmlDriver -convert MARC8 -normalize
  -out output.xml input.mrc
```

This command converts a file containing MARC 21 records to MODS. It uses the XSLT stylesheet provided by the Library of Congress. The MARC-8 ANSEL character data is converted to normalized UTF-8:

```
java org.marc4j.util.MarcXmlDriver -convert MARC8 -normalize
  -xsl http://www.loc.gov/standards/mods/v3/MARC21slim2MODS3.xsl
  -out output.xml input.mrc
```

XML Back to MARC

The `org.marc4j.util.XmlMarcDriver` requires an input file containing MARCXML. In addition the class takes zero or more of the following options:

-usage
> Show the usage text.

-out *output-file*
> Specify the name of the output file. If this argument is not present output is written to the console.

-convert *encoding*
> Convert the data elements from UTF-8 back to the given encoding. MARC4J supports the following encodings:
>
> - *MARC8* (MARC-8 ANSEL used by MARC 21)
>
> - *ISO5426* (ISO 5426 used by UNIMARC records)
>
> - *ISO6937* (ISO 6937 used by UNIMARC records)

-encoding
> Create output using the given character encoding. Use Java encoding names such as UTF8 and ISO8859_1.

-xsl *stylesheet*
> Process the XML data source through the XSLT stylesheet located at the given URL. The stylesheet should produce well-formed MARCXML data.

The following command simply converts the given file with MARCXML data to MARC in ISO 2709 format and writes output to the "standard" output stream:

```
java org.marc4j.util.XmlMarcDriver input.xml
```

To write the result to a file, add a file name and optional path:

```
java org.marc4j.util.XmlMarcDriver -out output.mrc input.xml
```

To write UTF-8 encoded MARCXML to UTF-8 encoded MARC in ISO 2709 format:

```
java org.marc4j.util.XmlMarcDriver -encoding UTF8
  -out output.mrc input.xml
```

To convert MARCXML data encoded in UTF-8 to MARC-8 ANSEL add the **-convert** argument with the *MARC8* encoding value:

```
java org.marc4j.util.XmlMarcDriver -convert MARC8
  -out output.mrc input.xml
```

This command converts a file containing MODS data using the XSLT stylesheet provided by the Library of Congress to MARC in ISO 2709 format. The UTF-8 data is converted to MARC-8 ANSEL:

```
java org.marc4j.util.XmlMarcDriver -convert MARC8
  -xsl http://www.loc.gov/standards/marcxml/xslt/MODS2MARC21slim.xsl
  -out output.mrc input.xml
```

Indexing MARC with Lucene

The MARC4J Lucene API provides a command-line utility called `MarcIndexDriver` to populate a Lucene index with MARC data. Make sure to add `lucene-core-2.0.0.jar`, `marc4j-lucene.jar`, `marc4j.jar` and `commons-logging-1.1.jar` to your CLASSPATH environment variable. The `marc4j-lucene.jar` and `commons-logging-1.1.jar` packages are included in the download for the MARC4J Lucene API.

The `org.marc4j.lucene.util.MarcIndexDriver` requires an input file containing MARC records. In addition the class takes zero or more of the following options:

-usage
   Show the usage text.

-index *index-directory*
   Specify the name of the directory containing the Lucene index. If this argument is not present an in-memory index is created. On exit this index will be destroyed.

-create

    Create a Lucene index at the given index directory or overwrite the existing one.

Warning

This option will overwrite any existing index with a new one.

-schema *schema URL*

    Use the Lucene index schema located at the given URL. The schema document should conform to the MARC4J Indexing Schema DTD (see: Figure B.1, "Indexing Schema"). It is generated from a RELAX NG Schema. If this argument is not present the default index schema will be used. The default index schema is based on the MARC 21 to Dublin Core crosswalk.

Figure B.1. Indexing Schema

```
<?xml encoding="UTF-8"?>

<!ELEMENT document (field)+>

<!ELEMENT field (record|(leader?,(controlfield|datafield)*))>

<!ATTLIST field
  name CDATA #REQUIRED
  index (no|tokenized|untokenized) #REQUIRED
  store (compress|yes|no) #REQUIRED>

<!ELEMENT record EMPTY>

<!ELEMENT leader EMPTY>

<!ATTLIST leader
  start CDATA #REQUIRED
  end CDATA #IMPLIED>

<!ELEMENT controlfield EMPTY>

<!ATTLIST controlfield
  tag CDATA #REQUIRED
  start CDATA #IMPLIED
  end CDATA #IMPLIED>
```

```
<!ELEMENT datafield (subfield)+>

<!ATTLIST datafield
  tag CDATA #REQUIRED>

<!ELEMENT subfield (#PCDATA)>
```

The following command simply creates an in-memory index and indexes the MARC records in `input.mrc` using the default index schema:

```
java org.marc4j.lucene.util.MarcIndexDriver input.mrc
```

To create a new index on the file system, or overwrite an existing one, and add the MARC records in `input.mrc` using the default index schema:

```
java org.marc4j.lucene.util.MarcIndexDriver
  -index /Users/bpeters/Documents/workspace/sru/index
  -create input.mrc
```

To add the MARC records in `input.mrc` to an existing index using the default index schema:

```
java org.marc4j.lucene.util.MarcIndexDriver
  -index /Users/bpeters/Documents/workspace/sru/index input.mrc
```

This command adds the MARC records in `input.mrc` to an existing index using the given index schema:

```
java org.marc4j.lucene.util.MarcIndexDriver
  -index /Users/bpeters/Documents/workspace/sru/index
  -schema file:///Users/bpeters/Documents/workspace/sru/schema.xml
  input.mrc
```

References

Publications

Fowler, Martin. Patterns of Enterprise Application Architecture. Boston: Addison Wesley, 2003.

Friedl, Jeffrey E. F.. Mastering Regular Expressions. Sebastopol: O'Reilly, 2006.

Gospodnetic', Otis and Hatcher, Eric. Lucene in Action. Manning: Greenwich, 2005

Understanding Metadata. NISO Press 2004. Available from http://www.niso.org.

Bibliographic Standards

Dublin Core Metadata Initiative [http://dublincore.org/]

MARC 21 XML Schema [http://www.loc.gov/standards/marcxml/]

MARC Standards [http://www.loc.gov/marc/]

Metadata Object Description Schema (MODS) [http://www.loc.gov/standards/mods/]

OAI MARC XML [http://www.dlib.vt.edu/projects/OAi/marcxml/marcxml.html]

ONIX for Books [http://www.editeur.org/onix.html]

SRU (Search/Retrieve via URL) [http://www.loc.gov/standards/sru/]

UNIMARC [http://www.ifla.org/VI/3/p1996-1/sec-uni.htm]

Helpful Internet Pages

Apache Lucene [http://lucene.apache.org]

Apache Tomcat [http://tomcat.apache.org/]

Eclipse IDE [http://eclipse.org]

Luke - Lucene Index Toolbox [http://www.getopt.org/luke/]

Sun Developer Network [http://java.sun.com/]

www.ingramcontent.com/pod-product-compliance
Lightning Source LLC
LaVergne TN
LVHW062318060326
832902LV00013B/2298